bigger Balls

bigger **Balls**

The CFL and Overcoming the Canadian Inferiority Complex

Jeff Giles

WINDING
STAIR
PRESS

National Library of Canada Cataloguing in Publication Data

Giles, Jeffrey, 1954-
    Bigger balls : the CFL and overcoming the Canadian inferiority complex

Includes index.
ISBN 1-55366-083-8

1. Canadian Football League. I. Title.

GV948.G54 2001   796.335'64   C2001-901846-0

Winding Stair Press
An imprint of Stewart House Publishing Inc.
Etobicoke, Ontario
www.stewarthousepub.com

1   2   3   4   5   05   04   03   02   01

This book is available at special discounts for bulk purchases by groups or organizations for sales promotions, premiums, fundraising and educational purposes. For details, contact: Peter March, Stewart House Publishing Inc., Special Sales Department, 195 Allstate Parkway, Markham, Ontario. Tel: (866) 474-3478.

Printed and bound in Canada

Acknowledgements

I would like to thank my wife, Lee, who for the past twenty-one years has been there right beside me in the front car of the roller-coaster experiencing all the ups and downs and twists and turns with me. Her love and support, along with that of my kids, Lauren and Scott, has been incredible. Without them I'm not sure I would have made it through the last six years. I love you guys.

I would also like to thank my Dad for introducing me to the CFL when I was young and for continually providing me with sound fatherly advice and support when I needed it the most.

Contents

Acknowledgements

Foreword ix

1 The Journey 1

2 Why Bigger Balls and Why Now? 9

3 To Be or Not to Be…Canadian 16

4 Rules of the Game 24

5 Journey to the Edge of the Abyss, Stage One 33

6 Crumbling Foundations 42

7 What Is a Radical Canadian? 50

8 What It Takes to Be a Radical Canadian 57

9 Journey to the Edge of the Abyss, Stage Two 63

10 Is There a Limit to How Many Times
One Team Can Punt? 71

11 The Ottawa Money Pit 79

12 Balancing the Grey Cup 83

13   The 1997 Season: The Long Road Back   92

14   Behind the Scenes: Playing Politics   103

15   The 1998 Season: Competition Is a Great Thing   111

16   Behind the Scenes: The Politics Get Dirty   118

17   The 1999 Season: Wrestling with Opportunities   126

18   Eventco?   136

19   Behind the Scenes: The Politics Get Dirtier   145

20   The 2000 Season: In other Arenas   152

21   The Ottawa Initiative   159

22   The Search for a Strategic Partner...Again   169

23   Behind the Scenes: The Final Straw   172

24   A Radical Future   181

25   A Great Cause: The Source of Real Change   188

26   Lessons Learned on the Journey   197

     Index   209

Foreword

It has been suggested many times over the years that maybe Canada wasn't meant to be in the first place.

History, geography, environment and commerce, among other things, create a strong north-south pull which seems to magnify the challenges already present in building a nation north of the 49th parallel.

And yet, we have prevailed, creating not only a nation, but one of the most blessed, admired, and yes, successful nations in the world by almost any measure.

Many Canadians put this success down to the good fortune we have in being located next to the United States, the world's most powerful nation, and the world's biggest commercial market. To some extent, they're right, bringing to mind the old saying that "it's better to be lucky than smart."

But that suggestion sells our country short and sells us short as a people. Come to think of it, Canadians are the best short sellers in the world, not in the context of financial markets, but when it comes to a modesty, indeed an almost pathological sense of inferiority about ourselves, our country and things Canadian.

That may explain why we have also been prepared to let many of our Canadian institutions slip away over time. If you don't place much value on something, then you don't worry too much if it disappears. Being a relatively young country, we didn't have too many things to call our own to begin with.

I have always been a CFL fan. My two uncles, Al Stevenson and Ted Smith, took me to games starting when I was a very young boy. My father was also a fan but felt (correctly) in those days that attending games in person at the old Exhibition Stadium in Toronto was best suited to those who were young and foolish, or older and well fortified by liquid refreshment. He was neither.

Some 25 years later, when I was asked by former Ontario Premier Bill Davis and current Ontario Chief Justice Roy McMurtry (both former Chairmen of the CFL) to become the lawyer for the league, I thought this was a perfect way to combine a profession with a passion. Little did I know that the passion would make it the start of an odyssey that lasted for more than a decade.

The CFL is one of those rare Canadian institutions, and it has seemed in some danger of slipping away throughout its history. At first, I viewed that fragility with a certain degree of professional concern, but as time went on, and matters got worse, the passion did indeed begin to emerge and I was determined to lead the process of seeing the CFL strengthened and preserved.

My reasoning was very simple. If we have something here that is part of the historical Canadian tradition, a game itself that is uniquely Canadian, played in cities across the land, with the majority of players being Canadian, then that in and of itself was worth preserving.

If people in Prince Albert thought the game and the league worthy of driving for hours and hours to get to a Roughrider game, then it was worth preserving.

If fans in Edmonton, Calgary and Winnipeg would come out to cheer on their teams in a raging blizzard, then it was worth preserving.

If Ticat fans in Hamilton kept coming out even when the ravages of recession made it almost impossible, then it was worth preserving.

Indeed it was, and it is, and this book by Jeff Giles, one of those most instrumental in the rebuilding of the CFL, chronicles the ups and the downs, the trials and the tribulations that saw the CFL go from death's door and back to respectability during the late 1990s. As you will read, Jeff's role was often controversial, but his steadfast commitment was never in question.

But the book is about much more than that. It is also a thoughtful examination of that Canadian sense of modesty, of inferiority to which I referred earlier. And it's a wake up-call.

Quite properly, it calls on Canadians to get a bit emotional about their country. To show a bit of passion about what we have and what we are. To ask people to think about how good we are and how much better we can be, rather than putting ourselves down.

Jeff Giles is asking all Canadians to find their own CFL. Take on a challenge that will at one and the same time celebrate our citizenship and our nationhood, while making us just a little bit stronger in the process.

There will always be those who put down the CFL, just as there will always be those who put down Canada. That's what a democracy allows. But like Jeff Giles, I chose a different route, joining millions of fans, a dedicated league staff and a handful of incredibly dedicated and passionate owners and club officials to try to rebuild and strengthen a longstanding Canadian institution.

It was fun. You will read the stories in this book and laugh. Hopefully, you will also read this book and be proud, be inspired to do something for Canada, whether it is something on the street where you live or something which goes beyond. Buying a ticket to a CFL game near you would surely qualify!

John Tory
Toronto, June 2001

1

The Journey

It was a relatively mild Saturday for the end of November. Tens of thousands of people of all ages lined the parade route, waiting to see the floats and marching bands. The atmosphere was festive and electric – but I suspected that no one would be too impressed by the management-type clown riding along in a convertible with his family. After six long, sometimes hair-raising years in the Canadian Football League, I was honoured that the organizing committee for the 2000 Calgary Grey Cup parade had included me in the festivities. I just wasn't sure how the fans would feel.

Much to my surprise, the reception these parade-goers gave me and my family was overwhelmingly warm. Along the way, hundreds yelled out, "Thanks, Jeff," while many more showed their appreciation with applause or a friendly wave. It was gratifying to know that so many people appreciated our efforts, and it was encouraging to be reminded that Canadian businesses — like the CFL — continue to occupy a very special place in the hearts of most Canadians. The parade also reminded me how much I had changed over the past six years — my experience with Canadian football had stirred in me an emotion that I had been missing before: Canadian spirit.

When people learn of my involvement with the CFL, they automatically assume that working in sports was something I always wanted to do. Not true. In fact, making a living in the wacky and unpredictable world of professional sport had not even entered my mind until one morning in the fall of 1994. I was deeply immersed in my job as the chief financial officer of a large retailer when a co-worker walked into my office with an ad torn out of the *Globe and Mail*. He threw it on my desk and, with just a hint of sarcasm in his voice, said, "Here's the job for you."

After scanning the ad for chief operating officer/chief financial officer for the Canadian Football League, I looked up and said, "You have to be kidding." It was widely known that the state of the CFL was precarious at best. The general perception among those who followed sports in Canada was that it was a lost cause, a dinosaur on the edge of extinction. In my quick read of the advertisement, I was surprised to see how closely the requirements matched my experience and strengths. The opportunity intrigued me. But I didn't want to risk embarrassment by letting on, so I pretended to dismiss the idea outright.

Later, alone in my office, I read the ad again, this time in a little more detail. I found myself starting to play the "what if?" game in my head. After a few minutes of thought, during which I came up with far more reasonable questions than reasonable answers, I put the ad in my desk drawer, where it would now be out of sight but certainly not out of mind.

People who know me well know that I've never been one to shy away from a challenge. I cut my teeth as a chartered accountant working in the highly volatile bankruptcy and insolvency business and then moved on to various turn-around and start-up situations, all laced with a great deal of uncertainty and risk. At the time when the CFL ad was thrown on my desk, I was just completing the third year of a very successful turnaround in the retail industry, and I was already starting to think about my next challenge.

Although my tolerance for risk may be slightly higher than average, I must admit that the CFL made me quite nervous. It's one thing to take on a huge challenge in relative obscurity; it's quite another to do so in the public eye. I had followed the CFL enough to know that despite its private ownership structure, it is in effect a very public organization — one that attracts more than its fair share of attention and scrutiny from both media and fans.

But at some point while I was considering employment with the CFL, my curiosity and competitive nature simply got the better of me: I decided to apply. I got an initial interview, and then a second one. Throughout the three- or four-week interviewing period, I bounced around the idea of working for the CFL with various friends and relatives, consistently getting a response that could best be described as lukewarm. Their reaction didn't really bother me all that much, since I had grown accustomed to this kind of reception to my career choices. I did sense, however, that the lack of enthusiasm for this opportunity was a little more intense than usual. Even my dad, who had always been a big CFL fan and a major source of support for me over the years, was unusually guarded with his comments. Yet the more people protested, the more I wanted the job. Despite public risk, I could think only of the challenge.

My motivation was heightened by my personal memories of the CFL. I couldn't help but reminisce about my days as a youngster in Ottawa, when I would sneak over to Lansdown Park and watch my beloved Rough Riders practise. I thought back to those times when my dad took me to the games and we would cheer so loudly that we lost our voices. I remembered sitting around the TV on Grey Cup Sunday with my entire family, cheering for whatever eastern team was playing, and eating until we couldn't eat any more. In the end, the tug of those memories, combined with the thrill of a challenge, overrode any concerns about the future of the league, the relative instability of the job, or any personal career risks. At some point, the opportunity transformed itself from a simple job into a personal cause. Maybe I was a little naive, but I thought I could make a difference and I wanted the opportunity to prove it.

But as often happens, after I had talked myself into the job, the league decided to offer the position to another candidate. Perhaps trying to spare my feelings, the headhunter told me I was a close second. I was devastated. When I told my friends and family, they could sense my disappointment and so they tried to be sympathetic. Most likely they were suppressing a deep sense of relief. Then, about three weeks later, fate stepped in: the headhunter called to say that they couldn't reach an agreement with the first candidate. He wanted to know if I was still interested, and the league agreed to negotiate with me exclusively. As they say, the rest is history.

I didn't know it at the time, but the emotional roller coaster that I rode between the time I first saw the advertisement and the time I finally got the job was nothing compared to the ride that I was about to take. In light of the very public personal challenges and attacks I endured in my time with the CFL, people often ask me if I have any regrets about taking the job. My answer is never. Sure, there were times when I questioned whether all the stress and aggravation were worth it, but fortunately those times were few and far between. And when those moments did occur, inevitably something would happen to remind me why I had wanted the job in the first place, which was just to make a difference.

Two recent encounters, for example, will stay with me forever. The first was Michael "Pinball" Clemons's final game
at SkyDome in the fall of 2000. Close to 30,000 people
showed up to say farewell to one of the most popular players
ever to play this game and wish him well as he embarked on
his new coaching career with the Toronto Argonauts. After
the game, CFL chairman John Tory and I made a presentation to Pinball at centre field. When it came time for Pinball
to speak, he took the microphone and made a few remarks to
the fans. He then walked over to John and me and, in front
of all 30,000 people, thanked us personally for first saving
and then revitalizing the league. Those words, coming from
a player of Pinball's esteem, meant more to me than I can
express. It was gratifying and humbling to know that I had
earned the respect of Pinball and, by association, other players across the league.

Another moment came at the 2000 Grey Cup when, after
the parade, I had the opportunity to flip the game coin at
centre field. The emotion of the time and place was almost
palpable; I waited with Dave Yule, head official, and watched
the world-renowned Snowbirds fly overhead to salute the
crowd. The B.C. Lions were the first to arrive at centre field
for the toss. Several of the Lions, including Lui Passaglia,
shook my hand and thanked me for my hard work. The fact
that these players took the time to recognize my contribution at such a significant moment in their own careers was
truly flattering.

Even more than contact with great people, my involvement with the CFL has given me the opportunity to learn a lot about myself. I have begun to truly appreciate what it means to be a part of this country, and for that I will always be grateful. I'll admit that when I joined the CFL, I was a passive, somewhat apathetic Canadian. When it came right down to it, despite all my vivid memories of Canadian football, I saw the CFL as just another struggling business that needed fixing. Not concerned about separatism or the Americanization of our country, I never worried about issues of Canadian pride or Canadian heart in relation to business. If our institutions and traditions were on the decline, then I assumed it was meant to be. I also assumed (incorrectly) that if these developments were against our best interests, someone would be protesting on our behalf. Even if I did disagree with the deterioration of Canadian traditions, I didn't think there was much that I could do to change things.

My awareness of Canadian pride and heart grew when my role in the CFL brought them into focus. Because sport embodies tradition and pride, it made me think about what affects national pride. I began to appreciate just how lucky we are to live here, just as I felt an increasing concern for what was happening – or, in some cases, not happening – in our country. Eventually that concern grew into frustration and anger. Most Canadians have no idea how lucky they are to live in Canada. As a result, most Canadians also don't seem to appreciate just how fragile our country is, how vulnerable our businesses are, how much we have already lost, or how much more we will lose if this erosion continues unchecked.

Through my experiences in the CFL, I have come to realize that many Canadians have very little self-confidence. For a nation full of talented people, this is an alarming situation – one that, in some sectors, has created a huge inferiority complex. We need to embrace change both in attitude and in action, and we need to do it now. This requires courage. To adapt the CFL's Radically Canadian slogan, we need bigger balls, and we need them now. Not just for the sake of the CFL, but for the sake of our whole country.

2

Why Bigger Balls and Why Now?

I often daydreamed about writing a book that would stir
up public debate and result in developing some real solutions to help rebuild the CFL. Initially, I was simply thinking about the league as a business. But as my appreciation
for the game and its place in Canadian culture grew, my
goals for this imaginary book expanded. I became aware that
most people who really care about this game are also passionate nationalists, who will bleed profusely Canadian red
when only lightly scratched. For these people (and I now
include myself in this group), it is impossible to debate the
future of the CFL in isolation from the deeper issues facing
our country, such as the growing Americanization of our
culture. The CFL is, after all, a Canadian business struggling
with the same problems as every other business in this
country. The problems are similar and so are the solutions.

Our country faces many challenges in light of globalization, technological advancement, and social trends. In particular, we as Canadians have created our own challenge by endorsing an environment that allows others to change the face of our country without our approval — to steal from us the very essence of being Canadian. To regain control, Canadians and Canadian businesses like the CFL must forge bold new visions and create aggressive new strategies. Most business people will tell you that effective strategies and tactics come from both research and past experiences. The CFL has always been a little short on good research, but it has never lacked for interesting experiences or battle scars that can teach all Canadians valuable lessons. These lessons should be applied to generate new solutions and should motivate all of us to take action and positively influence the things that are important to us. I hope that one of these things is the CFL.

Because of the CFL, I have travelled extensively across most of Canada and experienced first-hand the various attitudes and regional differences that make this country unique. In the process, I've spoken with thousands of passionate CFL fans, who were all eager to share their views and take me to task for the way we were running their league. I've verbally jousted with many an aggressive reporter. I've defended the league from the growing numbers of Canadians who despise the CFL, love the National Football League, and will state right to your face that their dream is to see the CFL disappear. I've pitched the benefits of the CFL in many a Canadian boardroom, some friendly and some anything but. And I've fought tooth and nail to overcome the petty politics within the CFL that obstructed any real change.

I've seen the good, the bad, and the ugly side of Canadians. My experiences have given me a crash course in Canadian culture that would rival anything taught in our universities. The CFL gets into your blood, not just for the game, but also for the level of emotion it elicits from people across the country. Those who believe in this game preach its benefits with a zeal that borders on evangelical – their enthusiasm is infectious. Those who are against it are just as emphatic and emotional. It's almost impossible not to get caught up in the debate, and when you do, it's in your blood forever – whether you like it or not. From a personal point of view, I am very concerned about Canada and the crossroads at which it finds itself. So, in an effort to put those emotions, experiences, and observations into perspective, I began to read as much as I could on the subject of Canada and its future.

We all know that Canada shares a border with one of the most powerful and ambitious nations in the world. The two neighbours have lived side by side in relative peace for centuries, proudly sharing the longest undefended border in the world. With the physical security that comes from such a relationship, Canada has built a country that is the envy of many around the world. It is rich in tradition and in a heritage that reflects the values of its people. These values include honesty, fairness, equal treatment for all, and a deep appreciation for the things that make us unique.

Despite this success, Canadians joke that we are probably the only group in the world who would question the results of a study that recently rated Canada as one of the best countries in the world in which to live. We look at each other and ask, How can this be? This insecurity is the price we pay for living next to such a loud, boastful country. Perhaps more as a defensive mechanism than anything else, Canadians have sought out and proudly clung to those things that clearly differentiate us from Americans – such as our social-security system, which includes education and health care for all, our liberal immigration policies, and gun control. It has been argued that Canada's quest to be unique has been driven more by what we didn't want to be – American – than by the desire to create our own identity and vision.

A brief illustration of this point: in early 2000, there were some unsubstantiated rumours that the CFL was considering changing from the traditional Canadian three downs to the NFL-regulation four downs. I never suggested that we were seriously considering this change, but I didn't come out and say it was off the table either. Essentially, I wanted to find out how much Canadians really cared about the league and why. On one hand, we received a great deal of constructive feedback that we later used in developing a new strategic plan. On the other hand, many people left me messages and sent letters suggesting that such talk was the equivalent of treason. I received a number of threatening phone calls from people who said that they would hound me for the rest of my life if we ever changed our rules. There were even two separate bomb scares. This was no longer an objective debate about a sport. Somehow, three-down football had clearly taken on a meaning well beyond the simple rules of a game.

So, we are "other than American," and in the past this strategy has not harmed us; we have a high standard of living and a worldwide reputation for being a great place to live. The question, however, is whether this strategy is the right one for the future. To continue playing a one-sided – defensive – strategy in light of the globalization and trade debates occurring all around us is shortsighted. I believe it is time for a new, proactive strategy. A strategy that will allow us to compete on a level playing field with everyone else and allow Canada to control its own future.

For the past 20 years or more, many Canadians have watched in frustration as American and other foreign companies have either bought up our major corporations or, worse, put them out of business through competition. At the same time, we have seen our unique cultural identity slowly erode under the pressure of the U.S.-dominated media, which has penetrated our country to an unprecedented level. One of those important cultural treasures that we've lost control of is the game of hockey, the very game that we invented. Americans now control the National Hockey league; we've lost two NHL franchises to the Americans so far, and the likelihood is that we will lose more. As a direct result of many similar, larger-scale economic and cultural losses, our standard of living has silently and rapidly been falling behind that of our neighbour to the south – a fact of which most Canadians are completely unaware. This silent erosion has been massive in scale and, in many cases, irreversible.

It has been suggested that the North American Free Trade Agreement, which went into effect on January 1, 1994, is about to evolve into a Common Market agreement, similar to the one that has been in existence in Europe for years. A Common Market agreement will expand on the free movement of product as provided for by NAFTA and add the free movement of both labour and capital. The experts tell us that this is sure to spell the end of the Canadian dollar, which will also likely mean the end of any control over our fiscal or monetary policies.

I can hear some people saying that this could never happen in Canada. But the realist in me argues otherwise. It happened in Europe, and recently our own prime minister advised Canadians not to be afraid of becoming citizens of the world. Does this mean, then, that an organization like the CFL should think globally, rather than nationally? Is it not reasonable to expect the competition to invade what we used to believe was our exclusive territory?

Research shows that Canada is a very divided country. This contention was certainly supported by the results of the 2000 federal election, in which the country split itself into three distinct political factions. Generally speaking, Ontario went Liberal, the West supported the Alliance party, and Quebec split itself between the Liberals and the Bloc Québécois. This division is a major problem for our country, and I believe it threatens our very existence.

While diversity is an asset, it brings with it certain challenges. After all, if there really isn't such a thing as an average Canadian, is it possible to have a unified vision? In part, our diversity is related to the size of our country, the effects of immigration, and the obvious language issues that separate Quebec from the rest of Canada. Less obvious, but very evident within the CFL, are the issues that separate western Canada from eastern Canada, the general animosity felt toward Ontario, the specific dislike for the city of Toronto, and the sense of neglect felt by people in the Maritimes. Mix in the effects of our constant exposure to U.S. media and the propensity to believe that anything American is better, and the result is a country divided along nationalistic, emotional, geographical, ethnic, economic, and linguistic lines. As you might imagine, this diversity represents a tremendous challenge for any business trying to market and sell its product. It also represents a challenge for those who have the courage to try to forge a much-needed unified cultural vision. I believe that the solution is to welcome our differences, while focusing on what we have in common, and build from there.

3

To Be or Not to Be...Canadian

A recent national poll asked Canadians to define what makes us Canadian. The answer was far from clear. Conducted by *Maclean's* magazine and published in December 1999, the poll highlighted, among other things, the fact that Canadians continue to have a strong sense of identity. The problem arose when respondents were asked to be specific. The most popular answer, selected from a list of factors that make Canada unique, was our flag. Following closely in second place was the achievements of prominent artists and scientists, and in third was our climate and geography. Not until the fourth most popular answer – health care – do we find a difference of real substance.

Most people would expect our health-care system to rank up near the top of the poll, but to rank the flag ahead of bilingualism, our multicultural population, or our belief in equal treatment for the poor and disadvantaged is a sad statement. Our flag is, indeed, a great flag, but rating it first is the equivalent of saying that the primary difference between two people is the colour of their hair. If we really believe that the main factor that distinguishes Canada from other countries is our flag, then perhaps we're not as unique as we think. (For the record, our multicultural society ranked 6th, bilingualism 9th, and our treatment of the poor 14th.)

The more American Canada becomes, the more difficult it is for Canadians to identify real differences between the two countries. What really make us special and different are our core values and ideals, such as equality for all in terms of health care and education, tolerance for others' points of view, and choosing negotiation over coercion. It is these values that form the core of the Canadian spirit – the spirit that unfortunately many Canadians seem to have neglected.

But spirit isn't the only thing we've forgotten; it seems we've lost sight of our southern neighbour as well. Over 66 percent of Canadians polled believed that our standard of living was higher than that of Americans. This certainly sounds good, and if it were true, it would be something to be proud of. Unfortunately, it's not true. In fact, in purely economic terms, not only do Americans enjoy a higher standard of living, but Canadians are continuing to fall farther behind.

An earlier poll, conducted in February 1998 by Goldfarb Consultants and printed in *Maclean's*, provided additional evidence of Canadian complacency. In this poll, Canadians were asked to place in order, from a list of national institutions and icons, the ones that helped them define being Canadian. In first place was the Order of Canada, followed in second place by the beaver. Tied for third with health care was the Canadian Football League, much-maligned and believed by many to be on the verge of extinction. When the poll came out, many in the CFL took these results as a positive sign for the league. I didn't share this view. It didn't make sense for the CFL to be ranked so far ahead of hockey, not to mention so far ahead of anything else.

I believed that the people polled were confirming that the CFL does have a lot in common with Canada, but not for the reasons we think. The similarities may have more to do with common struggles than common successes. My experience with the CFL has provided me with a unique perspective on this. As I see it, both our country and the CFL have long and distinguished histories, but both grapple with the conflict between the need to change to become relevant in the future and the desire to maintain the traditions of the past. Their supporters also share the same attachment to immaterial icons. Certainly to suggest that three downs, the way we pronounce the letter *z*, or our fondness for the beaver are important aspects of being Canadian is a half-hearted response, and is at the root of our recent inabilities to adapt.

The December 1999 *Maclean's* poll asked Canadians what they believed had to change to ensure that we keep our unique identity. The most popular answer, selected by 83 percent of the respondents, was the maintenance of Canadian ownership of our businesses. Close behind was the development of an entrepreneurial spirit, and in third, at 73 percent, was a willingness to take risks. These responses support the idea that we need to become more aggressive. Being entrepreneurial is all about going out on a limb, taking risks, and not being satisfied with the status quo. It's obvious that Canadians realize that we need to make some changes in order to preserve our identity. The question is, How do we start this change and who will lead the charge?

In this age of globalization, Canadians need to stop worrying about becoming American and focus instead on doing what we do well. Let's stop worrying about what we might lose and get passionate about what we want to become. Let's make sure that Canada remains an integral member of the new global village and that those attributes that make us uniquely Canadian not only survive but influence the development of this village.

I am convinced that the success of the new Montreal Alouettes franchise in the last few years has as much to do with pride, patriotism, and passion for uniquely Quebec properties as it does with good marketing or even a winning team. But then again, that's what good marketing is all about: identifying consumers' hot buttons and giving those consumers what they want. The Montreal organization should be congratulated for branding their product as Quebec's team and making sure the people of Quebec could identify with it. Their success should provide some guidance for other CFL teams and other Canadian businesses.

The challenge is to conquer our fears and insecurity and create a bold, courageous vision that reaches beyond our traditional borders and into the world market. The ongoing globalization of our economy, combined with the effects of technological change, has created a situation that requires us to reach out now or risk losing everything that we hold dear. Yes, this will require a change in the way we do business and, yes, we may have to consider changing certain things that we consider uniquely ours, or taking risks – but it doesn't mean that we have to change who we are. When it comes right down to it, being Canadian is about a unique spirit that we all share. It's this spirit that we should work at preserving, not the material things that we believe reflect this spirit. Learning to package, sell, and export this spirit is the key to our future.

For the CFL, this means coming to grips with the fact that, in the long term, the league cannot continue the way it is and hope to survive. No one would expect a company that makes and sells computers exclusively in Canada to compete successfully against Dell and IBM, so why do people think that the CFL should be able to compete against large-audience leagues by marketing only to Canada's population? A choice has to be made. The first alternative is to cut way back, turn the CFL into a semi-professional league that plays exclusively in Canada and hope for the best. The second choice is to expand the league in Canada and beyond, enhancing its appeal and creating something that we can all be proud of. I believe we owe it to the people who built this great Canadian game to ensure that its spirit survives and prospers.

The good news is that it may not be too late – there is reason for optimism. According to Allan R. Gregg, chairman of the polling firm The Strategic Counsel, a new voice is shaping our future, one which has not been at the forefront before. This voice is made up of women, young people, and our society's have-nots, who care deeply about health care, education, the environment, and the plight of the less fortunate. According to Gregg, these people are concerned not with what the future holds but rather with what they want to preserve from our past. I believe they have a point in that we have very little control over the future. Globalization is going to happen whether we like it or not. The growth of the Internet will make the world a much more intimate place, eliminating all borders, and there is nothing we can do about it. We must accept the fact that we can't control the future, but we *can* control what we preserve on the way – and the kind of people we want to be when we get there.

As individuals, we must also encourage our businesses to overcome their disabilities and get into the game. Thomas d'Aquino, president of the Business Council on National

Issues, recently gave a speech outlining what he believes are the shortcomings of corporate Canada. He, like the respondents in the *Maclean's* poll, focused on a lack of entrepreneurship, as well as a willingness to hide behind the weak Canadian dollar, as an excuse for poor performance. In his view, Canadian businesses also suffer from a hesitancy to reach out into foreign markets, a step that is critical to growth and long-term success in the new economy. A survey conducted by his organization found a deep frustration and an underlying attitude of envy among most Canadian organizations — the same envy shared by many Canadians on a personal level.

To further support this view, Ted Lyman, senior vice president of ICF Consulting, conducted a survey of the Ottawa high-tech sector and found that most companies lacked the "fire in the belly," the "let's bet the farm on this idea" mentality needed to be really successful. Lyman went on to say that if Canadian entrepreneurs really want to be a force in the corporate world, they must accept certain failures not as a stain of shame but as a badge of boldness.

What this country needs is a grassroots revolution. A revolution led by people who care and who have the courage to stand up and acknowledge that they are upset with the way things are going. People who have that "fire in the belly." People who are prepared to climb way out on a limb while others watch safely from the ground. The challenges faced by this country require far more leaders than we currently have, and I firmly believe that there are lots of Canadians who really want to be leaders. There are people at every level of our society who have the skills to become leaders. I am not talking about just the corporate elite, for a true revolution doesn't start at the top but at the bottom. It can start with a well-organized group, or it can start with one person with a cause. It can start with you, a Radical Canadian.

To become a successful revolutionary and ultimately a Radical Canadian, you need to identify your particular cause and then be a leader for it. Radical Canadianism is a challenge to the average Canadian to step up and be counted. I'm hoping that this book will spark innovation in a new generation of passionate leaders.

4

Rules of the Game

To play any game effectively, to successfully implement new
strategies, you have to know the rules, whether it's in sports,
business or any other activity. Understanding the rules, however, isn't always enough. To truly be successful, it is also
necessary to understand the subtleties of the game, including its history. This is true for the CFL, and I belive it holds
true for most other Canadian business as well.

To the untrained eye, Canadian and U.S. football look
very much alike – because they evolved from the same
British game. They both have the same goal: to move the
ball by running it or passing it into the end zones. Both
versions of football are played on large fields with goal
posts, end zones, and white field lines at five-yard intervals.
Both games begin with kickoffs and both games involve
punting (kicking) when the teams haven't achieved the
necessary yardage to retain possession of the ball. There

are players who play defence, a different set of players who play offence, and a mix of players who play on the special teams (those involved in punting or kicking plays). Games are split into four quarters of 15 minutes each, with a half-time break when the players go to the dressing rooms for a brief rest.

But although the basics – throwing, tackling, blocking, and kicking – are the same, notable differences exist, providing an excellent example of the game's evolution over time. Football as we know it in North America started when a young British soccer player decided to pick up the ball and run with it, committing a flagrant violation of the rules. This was 1823, and the game came to be called rugby football, after the player's school: Rugby. (In Britain, soccer was, and is, known as football.) This radical young soccer player managed to start a new game, one that allowed the players to both carry and kick the ball according to certain rules. The game grew in popularity, and in 1871 the Rugby Football Union was formed and established itself as Britain's governing body for the sport.

The new British game made its way across the Atlantic and became increasingly popular at universities in Canada and the eastern United States. According to Canadian historians, the first football game was played at the University of Toronto on Saturday, November 9, 1861. (The first written account of a football game was of a match held at Montreal's McGill University in 1868.) According to U.S. historians, the first college game played in the United States didn't occur until 1869, when Princeton played Rutgers.

As the game grew in both countries, the rules continued to undergo tremendous change. Although there were attempts to keep the rules consistent on both sides of the border, each country basically developed its own rules. The result was the development of two distinct games. There is perhaps no other major sport where the rules vary as much as they do between the Canadian version of professional football and the American one. If a similar situation was to present itself today, the communication technologies now available to us would make such an outcome unlikely. But in the late 1800s and early 1900s, correspondence between (and indeed within) the two countries was more difficult and transportation was onerous at best. So while the Canadians worried about making their rules the same across the country, the United States went about doing the same, with distinctly different results.

In 1891, the Canadian Rugby Union was established, and from then on it continued to adapt the rules of the game. In that first year, the CRU adopted a number of rules that are still used today in the CFL, including the requirement that a team must gain 10 yards in three downs in order to retain possession of the ball, and the requirement that there be at least 1 yard between the two opposing lines. The most dramatic rule change came about in 1931, when the forward pass was approved. Until then, teams were allowed to pass the ball only backward or laterally, which was a throwback (pun intended) to rugby rules. In 1936, the CRU decided that teams would be allowed to use up to five imported players, which was the first real step toward preserving Canadian football for Canadians.

Meanwhile, the U.S. wrote and adopted its first rules in 1876. Walter Camp became the leading figure in rules development and is generally referred to as the "father of American football." Under Camp's guidance, the next decade saw a variety of rule changes including a reduction in the number of players. At one time there were 15 players per team; this was reduced to 11, the number used today in the NFL. The requirement to advance the ball by at least 5 yards in three downs or less in order to maintain possession was implemented. At some point in that same decade, U.S. rulemakers decided to change the number of downs to four and the yards required to 10, thus creating one of the major variances between the Canadian and the American game.

For those not familiar with football, the term "down" can be confusing. Simply stated, a down is nothing more than a "try" for points, and each play is considered a separate try. In the CFL, a team has three tries (or less) to gain 10 yards or more. If the players succeed, then they get a new set of three downs to cover another 10 yards or more. This process continues until the team crosses the goal line, which is called a touchdown, or until it gets close enough to kick a field goal. If the team doesn't reach 10 yards in three tries, then the other team takes over at the spot where the first team was stopped.

In both leagues, if a team isn't certain it can achieve 10 yards, players will use their last down to kick or, as they say, punt the ball to the other team. This is where the phrase, "If in doubt, punt," originates. What this means is that, in reality, the CFL teams have only two tries to get 10 yards, while the NFL teams get three tries. For this reason, there tends to be more passing in the CFL, as it is more difficult to run on a regular basis and get 10 yards in two tries. The extra down in the NFL lends itself to more running, which for the average fan is the most boring play in football. This is why the NFL is often described as "three downs and a cloud of dust" football — a direct reference to the perception that it involves more running plays. The additional passing in the CFL generally makes it a more exciting and unpredictable game.

Many believe that the third down punt is the most exciting play in the CFL. Unfortunately, the same cannot be said of the punt return in the NFL, due to another of the major rule variations between the two leagues. In the CFL, the team receiving the kick must catch or field the ball (unless it goes out of bounds) and try to return it. In the NFL, the receiving team is allowed to let the ball bounce until it is dead, or the receiver can simply wave his hand over his head before catching the ball. The latter is called a fair catch, which means that the ball is dead where he catches it, and no one is allowed to touch him. As a result of this rule variance, the punt return in the NFL is often a non-event, while in the CFL it is one of the most exciting plays.

The size of the field and number of men also make for a few main differences in play between the leagues. The NFL field is 50 yards wide and 100 yards long, with end zones 10 yards deep at either end. This brings the total field length to 120 yards. The CFL field is larger: 65 yards wide and 110 yards long, with end zones 20 yards deep. The CFL plays with 12 men on the field while the NFL plays with 11. In the CFL, even with one extra man, the added size of the field means that there's more turf to cover. This provides for a much more unpredictable game. The field is literally wide open.

Another difference between the leagues is speed. In the NFL, the teams have 45 seconds between plays before they must execute another play. CFL teams have only 20 seconds once the ball is placed. This means that there are generally more plays in a CFL game and less downtime for the fans. As a result of these major differences, the CFL has been called "longer, wider, faster football." While many other variations between the rules of the two games exist, there are two that, in my opinion, epitomize the CFL.

The first one is the requirement that about half the players must be Canadian. At the time of writing this, the CFL uses a 39-man active roster for each team, of which at least 19 players must be Canadian. To the best of my knowledge, the CFL is the only professional league anywhere in the world that insists that a certain number of places must be reserved for its citizens. Not only is this truly unique, but it also ensures that Canadian kids will have a place to play professional football. Without this rule, it is entirely possible that football could have disappeared from all Canadian universities by now.

The second rule isn't as significant as the Canadian quota, but it has become a focal point for many of the great arguments between CFL fans and NFL fans. In the CFL, when the ball goes through the end zone on either a punt or a missed field goal, the team kicking the ball is awarded one point. A team can also get a point if a player on the receiving team catches the ball and is tackled in the end zone. This is affectionately referred to as a "rouge." There is no equivalent in the NFL. Supporters of the NFL rule argue that a rouge is like awarding a point for failure, and supporters of the CFL rule say it creates exciting and unique plays. Neither side seems likely to change its mind.

What unified football in Canada was the donation by Lord Earl Grey in 1909 of a trophy that was to be awarded for the rugby football championship of Canada. To qualify, teams had to be registered with the Canadian Rugby Union. The jumble of regional associations now had a major incentive for national unification, and the trophy became known as the Grey Cup. It was first awarded in December of that year to the University of Toronto for defeating the Parkdale Canoe Club. The game was played in Toronto at the Rosedale Field before 3,807 fans.

Today, the strength of the CFL continues to be its champi-onship game, the Grey Cup. The 2000 Grey Cup game in Calgary was watched by, on average, almost 3.2 million viewers on CBC. The reach for that game, which calculates the total number of different Canadians who tuned in at some point, was in excess of 8 million. This is nearly one in three Canadians. Perhaps the Grey Cup has such a reach because it continues to be one of the last traditions that links us to an era when being Canadian was something to cele-brate regularly. Watching the Grey Cup game or being part of a Grey Cup party takes us back to a part of our heritage. For one Sunday every November, it gives us the opportunity to celebrate something that is still uniquely ours.

The Grey Cup was established a full 58 years before the first Super Bowl was played in 1967. Up until the early 1980s, from a business perspective, the CFL was arguably as strong as, if not stronger than, the NFL. In fact, at that point, CFL players made more than their NFL counterparts. But today there is no comparison. The NFL has grown in stature and size to the point where it is arguably the pre-eminent professional sports league in the world, and it has left the CFL in its dust. During its period of rapid growth (1967 to the 1990s), the NFL continued to add teams and build a marketing powerhouse. The CFL, for its part, was content to remain at eight teams and didn't see any reason to alter its low-key approach to sports marketing. Unfortunately, the spirit of that young British renegade soccer player didn't survive in Canada as it did in the United States. The NFL is now a force while the CFL is struggling to survive. Is there a lesson to be learned here?

It is my opinion that CFL football is a better game than the NFL version. As a result of the rules differences, it's much faster, less predictable, and more entertaining. Unfortunately, or fortunately, depending on your point of view, the hype around the Canadian game is much less, giving many people the impression that it's somehow an inferior product. This feeling of inferiority is augmented by those who naively belive that anything American just has to be better than the Canadian equivalent. In reality, nothing could be further from the truth, but as long as we as a nation continue to think this way about the CFL, or, for that matter, any other Canadian institution, business or product, the outcome will be self-fulfilling. Is that what we want?

5

Journey to the Edge of the Abyss, Stage One

When I joined the CFL in December 1994, its championship trophy, the Grey Cup, had been contested for over 80 years, although the CFL itself was not established until 1958. Now a federally registered, unincorporated association, the CFL is, in essence, owned by its members – the teams in the league – and a constitution dictates its management. Each club is represented by a governor (who is usually the owner of that team), and each team has one vote. The commissioner is the chief executive officer of the league, and the chairman runs the board meetings, representing the league when the commissioner is unable to do so.

Although the CFL is owned by its teams, I believe most people in the league feel themselves simply to be custodians of a great Canadian tradition that belongs to the people of Canada. This feeling is strongest among those teams that are community owned: Edmonton, Saskatchewan, and

Winnipeg. These teams are not-for-profit organizations, run by a voluntary board of directors for the people of their communities and represented on the CFL board by a governor chosen by the community. All the other teams are owned by for-profit companies.

At its peak, from the late 1970s to the mid-1980s, the league operated with nine teams. This changed in 1988 when the Montreal franchise pulled out, leaving the league with eight teams: Ottawa, Toronto, Hamilton, Winnipeg, Saskatchewan, Calgary, Edmonton, and B.C. During the last half of the 1980s, the league began a rapid decline in fan support and television audiences. The decline continued into the 1990s and, as a result, the CFL found itself in a desperate financial position. In response, the league made the bold decision to expand into the United States in order to survive, adding its first U.S. franchise in Sacramento in 1993. Baltimore, Las Vegas, and Shreveport were added to the mix for the 1994 season, which meant that the CFL now consisted of eight Canadian teams and four U.S. clubs.

My official start date was to be December 1, 1994, but the league graciously invited me and my wife to attend the Grey Cup in Vancouver the week before. I had never been to a Grey Cup game and I was extremely excited about the opportunity. It was the first time that an American club was to play a Canadian team for the right to our national title. My wife and I felt as though we were on a second honeymoon. We revelled in the festivities and the game, and we felt completely taken care of. I met many of the great legends of the game and many of the governors, who were quite friendly and very open. But things were not as they seemed with the league, although I didn't have any inkling at the time.

After returning to Toronto from Vancouver, I jumped into my new job with both feet. It didn't take long before I was hit with one of the first major shocks in a long line of shocks to come. After reviewing the books, I realized that the CFL had almost no cash or receivables — and that the one thing it did have was millions of dollars in current liabilities. In fact, we didn't have enough money to make payroll much past January 30. I remember going home and sharing this with my wife, who was also totally shocked. I'm not sure whether I was more upset with myself for not asking the right questions in advance or with the people who lured me away from a good job to work for a company with no money. Why had no one thought it was worth mentioning to me? At first I was angry that this information had been kept from me, but then I came to a sad realization: the fact that we were in this situation didn't seem to faze anyone. It was as if this were the normal course of business. That's when I realized this job was going to be more difficult than I had ever imagined.

The league's lack of cash wore on my mind throughout the entire Christmas holidays. There was some talk about selling a new franchise in January to save our bacon, but it

was far from a done deal. I went into my first board meeting in Edmonton on January 27, 1995, hoping to hear some
news that would make me feel better about my decision to
join the league. Unfortunately, most of what I learned only
added to my concern. It was reported that the Las Vegas
club was up for sale and there were no takers. The Sacramento team was looking to move after only two seasons.
And Bruce Firestone, the owner of the Ottawa club,
announced that his team was also up for sale. The only good
news came in the form of Arthur Williams, who presented
himself for consideration as the new owner of an expansion
franchise in Birmingham. The most encouraging part of
his presentation was the franchise fee that he was going to
pay – the largest ever in the history of the CFL.

We knew that Williams had a great deal of money. He
had just tried to buy the NFL's Tampa Bay Buccaneers for a
reported US$150 million but was unsuccessful for reasons
that were never made clear to us. I guess you could say we
got Williams on the rebound. I still don't know why he
wanted to buy a CFL club, except perhaps to show the NFL
that he was serious about football and that they had made a
mistake in turning him down. Since he had so much money,
the board was concerned that he might try to buy himself a
winner. In response to pointed questions on that topic he
confirmed that he would play by all the rules. My favourite
part of Williams's presentation was the way he said in his
southern drawl, " I looooove the CFL." The truth is that he

could have told us right to our faces that he was going to do something untoward and we would have still accepted him — we needed his money that badly. As they say, any port in a storm will do; and when you're desperate, any partner with money will do. Williams was accepted on the spot and his money was quickly deposited. For the next few months, we lived in relative calm.

On March 9, 1995, at the annual general meeting, it was announced that Memphis was also going to join the league and would begin play in less than four months. The owner was to be Fred Smith, the founder and CEO of Federal Express. Smith was somewhat of a revolutionary himself, having started Federal Express after doing a university thesis about an idea for overnight delivery of parcels. He proposed that every parcel in the United States would be picked up, delivered to one central location in the country, and then flown to its destination and delivered, all in less than 24 hours. Legend has it that the professor failed Smith because he thought the idea was impossible. To prove the professor wrong, Smith started Federal Express and got the best last word: success.

As it turned out, Fred Smith paid a lot less for his club than Arthur Williams had for the Birmingham club. Accepting less money made some sense at the time as Smith was, and still is, a very powerful and influential man who could help the CFL gain acceptance and credibility in the United States. This logic only made sense, of course, if you believed that Smith was getting involved because he really believed in and was committed to the CFL in the long term. We learned later that Memphis had been trying to get an NFL team for years, with no success. A cynical person might suggest that Smith had the same motivation as Williams. If this was indeed the case, then Smith got his message across to the NFL for a lot less money than Williams.

Pepper Rogers, who was to be the Memphis president and coach, represented the team at the March 9 meeting. In his career, he had coached at UCLA and the University of Memphis, as well as in the United States Football League, and he could best be described as a real character. By Rogers's own estimation, Memphis was a real hotbed for football. However, the main concern with the Memphis franchise had to do with the Liberty Bowl Stadium, where the team was to play its games.

The stadium held almost 60,000 people, but the field was far too small for a CFL playing surface. The NFL-sized field was grass, but the sidelines were Astroturf. To expand the field sideways to accommodate the larger CFL field meant that the last 3 yards on either side of the playing surface would extend onto the Astroturf. To make things worse, we could expand the NFL-sized end zones by only another 2 or 3 yards, which meant that instead of being 20 yards deep as in a regulation CFL field, they would be 13 yards deep – and they'd be on a severe slant, ending right at a large cement wall. When I first visited the field, my initial reaction was,

"What have we done?" I knew right away that this was going to come back to haunt us. Once again we were about to learn that when you're desperate, any idea seems like a good idea.

The March 9 meeting turned out to be one of the most famous in a long line of famous board meetings. Also in attendance was Jim Kelly, the de facto president of the Birmingham club and the right-hand man of the owner, Arthur Williams. It was common knowledge that the Birmingham club was in discussions with a well-known, experienced CFL quarterback who was a free agent at the time. Those on the inside also knew that this player was looking for a lot of money, much more than any club could afford and still stay within the league's salary cap. Even though Williams had been very emphatic only months before about his intention to play by the rules (and stay within the salary cap), there was a sense of foreboding in the room — a feeling that we were about to witness the beginning of the end.

Kelly came and went many times throughout the meeting, and it was obvious that something was up. At one point in the middle of the meeting, he returned and whispered something into the ear of his general manager, who was also the team's head of football operations. Despite the fact that a presentation was going on at the front of the room, every eye in the room was on Kelly as he whispered to the general manager. Those who were nearby strained to hear what was being said, while those farther away watched closely, trying to interpret the body language of the two men. Kelly stood up and asked the chairman if he could make an announcement. Kelly informed everyone that Birmingham had signed the quarterback in question. While no one knew at that time what the player's salary would be, there was a consensus that it was for a lot more than anyone else would have paid. The question we asked ourselves was: why?

With the benefit of hindsight, I believe this meeting in Saskatoon was one of the low points for our league and set the stage for the near-collapse to come. At the time, the league was in the process of finding new homes for two of its four existing U.S. teams. Despite this, we eagerly welcomed two new U.S. franchises, both located so far south that the people in the franchise cities barely knew where Canada was, let alone what the CFL was all about. The rift we would end up fighting was there from the very beginning.

In the midst of all this, Horn Chen had put an offer on the table for board approval. He wanted to purchase the Ottawa franchise, a club that had been recently abandoned by one of its former owners for the football-mad metropolis of Shreveport. The board approved the application to sell the historic franchise to Chen, a man who wasn't sure he wanted to be in Ottawa at all. We should have realized how fragile the situation was and focused on shoring up our existing business before we forged ahead with expansion.

The foundation of the league – the Canadian teams – was crumbling under all this weight, and yet we continued to build and add more. It's no wonder that the whole thing was about to come tumbling down.

6

Crumbling Foundations

Even with all of our problems, the 1995 season kicked off
just like the football season had for decades. In total we had
five U.S. teams – Baltimore, Shreveport, Birmingham,
Memphis, and San Antonio (the reincarnation of the old
Sacramento club) – along with eight clubs in Canada. But
as the season progressed, it became painfully obvious that
the U.S. experiment wasn't working. The crowds for most
clubs were dismal at best, with the exception of Baltimore,
where attendance averaged around 25,000 per game.
Despite these results, a false sense of security continued to
exist. The league was taking the power of positive thinking
to a whole new level. It seemed as though no one wanted to
face the obvious.

I attended a game in Ottawa against Memphis in August
1995 that illustrated the difficulties with the U.S. franchises.
From the sidelines between the two benches, I watched the

referee run over to the Memphis bench and address the coach, the infamous Pepper Rogers. The referee told the coach that for two successive punts his team had fielded only 11 players, rather than the 12 allowed. The coach turned to the referee and asked, "Is there a rule that says I can't play with eleven?" The response was no, so the coach yelled, "Well then fine, I'm going to play with eleven for the rest of the game, so leave me alone."

But although most of our focus was on the problems with the U.S. teams, there were also problems brewing in Canada. The Ottawa club, now under the ownership of Horn Chen (and his group of merry men), was not faring well; Winnipeg's debt, which had been growing for years, was reaching an unsustainable level; and Calgary, under the ownership of Larry Ryckman, was suffering tremendous financial stress. At each board meeting, it seemed that the teams were competing to see who had the most problems.

Somehow, someway, the league made it through the 1995 season and we celebrated one more year under our belts in Regina at the 83rd Grey Cup. This was the first time that the final had been played in Regina and, despite some fears that a city of its size might not be able to handle the event, it was one of the most successful Greg Cup games of all time. There was a truly festive atmosphere to the entire week, and all those who attended were very impressed. This game marked the first time that an American team had ever won the Cup. The Baltimore Stallions had made up for their loss in Vancouver the year before by beating the Calgary Stampeders. There was a lot of consternation over the Cup boarding the plane with the team and leaving Canada for the first time ever.

Another thing I remember about the game was that large temporary stands had been constructed in either end zone to increase the capacity of the stadium. The stands at one end were huge and seated almost 12,000 fans. As with any event of this nature, it was necessary to arrange for insurance and operate within the limitations of that coverage. The large stands were designed to carry the weight of 12,000 people – provided the winds were below a certain level, about 80 kilometres per hour. But by the time we were supposed to open the gates, the winds were gusting to over 90 kilometres per hour. We delayed the gate opening and monitored the situation closely. We had no idea what we would do if the winds didn't die down. To our relief, the winds did subside about an hour before the game and we were able to finally open the gates. The spectators, who didn't know what was going on, were annoyed with the delay. I assume they thought we had screwed up again. Needless to say, I spent the entire game with one eye on the field and one eye on the stands. I didn't relax until the game was over and everyone left safe and sound.

Shortly after the Regina Grey Cup, another historic board meeting was held in Toronto in November 1995, specifically to discuss the future of the U.S. clubs. Each club, including those in Canada, was asked to discuss its intentions for the 1996 season. Neither Birmingham nor Memphis was represented at the meeting, which I guess tells you every-thing you need to know about what their intentions were.

Five Canadian clubs said that they would definitely be playing in 1996. Two other teams – Calgary and Ottawa – indicated that they had some problems, but they were opti-mistic that they could continue. These responses were a little surprising, in light of the franchises' well-known financial troubles. We had all anticipated that the owners were going to announce that their teams were up for sale. However, the fact that they didn't sell turned out to be a real problem for us later.

The only real surprise for most of us came from B.C. The owner of the club had been the chairman of the executive committee and was very active in the league's affairs. His team had done well on the field, but was struggling off the field. Despite the club's problems, we never got the sense that the owner was unhappy – at least not until this meet-ing. He said that the losses were too high and that he wasn't sure what he was going to do. We were ready for the bad news from the U.S. clubs, but this development was unex-pected, and it hit us hard.

The first U.S. club to report was Baltimore, previously our most successful American team. We knew that the deci-sion by the Cleveland Browns to move their NFL franchise to Baltimore the next year was a death blow. As expected, the primary owner decided that it was best to look for a new home and he could not make a commitment for 1996 until he knew if the club had a place to play.

This news, combined with the apparent withdrawal of both Memphis and Birmingham, left the other two U.S. teams in a difficult situation. Fred Anderson, the owner of the San Antonio club, was visibly upset with the way things were going. Anderson was the one who brought the very first U.S. franchise into the CFL in 1993, when the Sacramento Gold Miners joined the league. He was a pioneer of sorts and was a very passionate and dedicated CFL supporter. He could sense that this meeting represented the end of something he had helped to start, and he was taking it very hard. Reluctantly, he said that he was not prepared to commit to the 1996 season and that he would make his final decision by the end of the year. It was as if he was delaying the inevitable as long as he could.

The only U.S. club that refused to accept its fate gracefully was Shreveport. There had been rumours that the club was making inquiries around Norfolk, Virginia, and the owner confirmed that they were going to abandon Shreveport and move to Virginia in 1996. The owner's son subsequently informed us that the team had already moved to Virginia and contracted to play in the stadium at Old Dominion University. He added that the team would be playing on a 100-yard field with 15-yard end zones, since that's all they could fit in the stadium. Not only that, but the club had already sold 1,400 season tickets. As you can imagine, the temperature in the room rose a few degrees very quickly at this evidence of the club's lack of concern for the other teams. The questions came fast and furious, and the other governors didn't pull their punches.

Over the next few months there were a number of meetings to update the board on the state of U.S. expansion – or, as it happened, contraction. The final board meeting with U.S. representatives was held in early February 1996. During the previous months, both Baltimore and San Antonio had expressed an interest in moving to Montreal. I'm not sure how the backroom politics worked, but in the end Baltimore and its two owners were given the nod. The most emotional moment of the day was when Fred Anderson spoke about the events that had led up to his involvement with the CFL and his wish that he could continue with the league. He was disappointed by losing the opportunity to relocate to Montreal and stated that he would love to return to the league if it was possible in the future. He then withdrew from the meeting amidst a round of appreciative applause.

Fred Anderson passed away a few years later, leaving a tremendous sense of loss with everyone who'd had the chance to know him. He was one of the nicest men that I've ever had the opportunity to know. Even today, five years after he pulled out of the CFL, there are still moments when I think of him and wonder what he would think of our situation today.

I personally believe that the decision to abandon the U.S. expansion initiative was the right one, given the circumstances. Having said that, I don't believe that the idea of U.S. expansion was wrong; in fact, I think that the CFL's future would be much improved by some form of U.S. presence. What was wrong with our foray was the timing and the execution. We did very little advance preparation and, as a result, there didn't seem to be any rhyme or reason to which cities were granted franchises. There was no real demographic research to see if the chosen locations suited the league, nor was there any analysis of the competition. For example, on the surface Birmingham seemed to be a football-crazy city and a perfect fit for the CFL. Once we got there, we quickly learned that very few people even knew where Canada was, much less what CFL football was about. Their passion for football was incredible, but it focused primarily on the rivalry between Auburn and Alabama, and after that on high school football. There wasn't much room left for that funny football played by those Canadians. This region of the United States is often referred to as the Bible belt; what others don't appreciate is that their devotion to American-style football is also a religion. To them, the CFL's style was blasphemous.

The U.S. expansion was motivated not by planning and foresight but by desperation. This caused the league to agree to deals that it probably never would have made otherwise. It also meant that there was no money to invest in marketing, promotion, or franchise development. If the league had been in a position to reinvest some portion of the franchise fees into rebuilding the business, there might have been a chance for success.

No one knows whether U.S. expansion might have worked under more ideal conditions. I only hope that we get another chance to find out. U.S. expansion is a very big and, dare I say it, Radically Canadian idea that just might be the future of this league. The key to making it work — both for the CFL and for other Canadian businesses — is to focus on our unique strengths and build from there, rather than being afraid of losing things that may not be so important after all.

7

What Is a Radical Canadian?

In 1996, after calling a halt to 3 years of U.S. expansion, the CFL limped back to Canada. After more than 100 years of professional football and over 80 Grey Cups, a mood of fatalism now hung in the air. We were going from a total of 13 teams back to 9 teams for the 1996 season. Many people in the media suggested that this would be the last season for the CFL and labelled the 1996 season the league's farewell tour. There was a feeling that Canadian-style football had become irrelevant in the new scheme of things. People pointed to the CFL as an example of a typical Canadian business that couldn't make it in the United States. At the same time, the country was struggling with the threat of Quebec separation, and a referendum was coming up later that year. There was a real sense of malaise throughout Canada.

I remember sitting down with a number of people within the CFL's head office and expressing my frustration with our situation. I was angry and I wanted to fight back. In an attempt to find a solution for the CFL, I took a look at what the other professional leagues in North America were doing. This only got me more upset, because I realized that without a lot more money there was no way we could implement anything close to what they were doing. The challenge for the CFL was to create a theme around which we could brand and promote the league, a theme that would communicate the fact that we were alive and well — and we had to do this with absolutely no money.

As we entered the planning process, there were only two things that I knew for sure. First, the theme had to centre on being Canadian; and second, it had to have an attitude. Other than that I had no ideas.

One day I was in the car with my family and I asked my kids for some words that they used to describe things that were cool. This was about the time that Don Cherry was hitting his stride as a hockey commentator, and one of his sayings was that "real Canadians" never stay down when they get hit. In his opinion, they get up off the ice under their own steam and go to the bench, but non-Canadians lie there until the trainer comes out to help. After some discussion about Don Cherry's great sayings, one of my kids suggested the word "radical." As soon as I heard it, I knew that was the word we were looking for. Our new slogan: "Radically Canadian."

Coming up with the slogan was one thing, but giving it

life was much more difficult. It was critical to properly define being Radically Canadian, or it was sure to fall flat. As I mentioned, it had to have an attitude and it had to deal with football, but I also wanted it to have a broader meaning. I knew I was taking a risk at the time, but I wanted Radically Canadian to be about more than football. I wanted it to stir national pride and passion, and I wanted it to be controversial. It had to be controversial in order to get noticed, because, without any money to advertise, we were going to need a lot of free publicity. The best way to get free publicity is to push the envelope.

During one of our many staff planning sessions, someone came up with the concept of selling merchandise to finance the campaign. As we were thinking of ideas for T-shirts, someone threw out the slogan "Our balls are bigger" — almost as a joke, never thinking that we would seriously consider it. The truth of the matter is that many years ago the CFL football was larger than the NFL ball; now, the two balls are exactly the same size. But I wasn't going to let technicalities get in the way of a good idea. I knew right then and there that this was the slogan that would bring the entire campaign to life. I'm sure everyone else thought I was crazy. The risks were substantial, but it was a chance worth taking and I was prepared to accept the consequences.

My initial concern was that the concept might be too over-the-edge for many of the more conservative people within the CFL, including many on the board. There was a good chance that, if the wrong people found out, the whole idea would be squashed before it even got off the ground. This is when I took my second big risk. I decided not to share the details of the idea with anyone on the board or with the commissioner, Larry Smith. I believed in what we were doing, but I wasn't sure that others would be prepared to take the risk with me. The best way to ensure that we had a chance was to keep the plan under wraps until we had reached the point of no return.

As we developed the campaign, we found ourselves getting carried away with ideas that we knew we couldn't afford. Some of the ideas were so good that we just had to find a way to finance them. One was the creation of a television commercial that would help define what Radically Canadian was all about. We had no idea how we were going to pay for it – all we knew was that we had to find a way. We did a little research and found out that those companies that sell knives that cut through steel, or that sell kitchen tools that slice and dice – these companies don't actually pay for their ads the traditional way. Instead, they pay the broadcaster a percentage of their sales. We created an ad that not only told our message but also sold merchandise. We then convinced a number of broadcasters to air the spot based on our projected sales.

By the time we created the commercial, designed the merchandise, put the infrastructure in place to handle sales and deliveries, and bought the merchandise, we were committed to over $250,000 in costs, with no guarantee that we would get a cent back. This was exactly $250,000 more than I was authorized to spend. I continued to keep the concept under wraps, for the reasons that I mentioned before and...fear. I was concerned that if anyone found out how much money I had risked without permission, my job would be on the line. For some organizations, $250,000 isn't much money, but for a league that was scraping together its nickels to pay the bills, it was a lot.

I presented the campaign to the governors at the June 1996 board meeting. The football season would begin in just weeks. Behind the scenes, the television commercials had been shot, the T-shirts and hats were made, and the print ads were ready to go. The meeting had not gone smoothly to this point. A number of surprise developments in the league meant that everyone was very upset and in a state of shock. The board was in no mood for any more controversy.

If there had been a choice, I probably would have postponed my presentation given the mood of the room, but the season was about to begin and the campaign was due to roll out in a few days. It was now or never. Somewhat reluctantly, I presented the Radically Canadian concept and the strategy behind it. I could see that most people were amused, which was probably the best reaction that I could have hoped for. Of course, I had yet to drop the "Our balls are bigger" bomb on them or reveal the amount that we had spent.

Before I did that, I gave them each a Radically Canadian golf shirt. They were so giddy, you would have thought that I'd just given them each $5,000. Someone made the tongue-in-cheek comment that this was the first time they had ever received anything from the league office. As everyone compared golf shirts, I slipped in the main slogans. The governors were so distracted by the events of the day and their free golf shirt that the "Our balls are bigger" slogan slipped through almost unnoticed. I found out later that a few people were so shocked that they didn't know what to say, so they said nothing. The lesson I learned from this experience is that it's not what you present that's important, but rather how and when you present it. For example, I never did tell them how much money I'd spent.

We launched the campaign in late June 1996, and the media's response was unbelievable. The headlines were all positive and the campaign was making the impression that we wanted. We generated a great deal of controversy, as we had hoped. It started with Quebec separatists, who took issue with the campaign and suggested that it was a ploy to work against separatism – which it was. Religious groups got upset with the "Our balls are bigger" slogan, suggesting that it was rude and vulgar. One team even refused to display the T-shirts, which only served to create greater demand. Overall, though, we managed to stir the deep-rooted Canadian pride in our game and in our country. When I went to the games I'd see the shirts throughout the crowd, proudly worn by fans making a statement. I knew we were successful the day I passed by a group of high school students in Toronto and saw one of them wearing one of the shirts. The best news for me personally was that we sold enough merchandise to more than recover our $250,000 — thank God.

8

What It Takes to Be a Radical Canadian

When we first launched Radically Canadian, we defined the
word radical as "to stand up with courage and passion against
great odds." Radically Canadian was about standing up for
our country and making a difference. It was about being
proud of our differences and celebrating our uniqueness. It
was about not having to apologize for being Canadian. In
essence, Radically Canadian was about being a revolutionary.

The term revolutionary may seem a little extreme, so let
me put it in context. When you think of a revolutionary,
there are many pictures that may come to mind, from a
swashbuckling hero who fights for freedom against great
odds, risking life and limb, to a thinker who changes the
world through invention or by creating a new political phi-
losophy. There is, however, another kind of revolutionary.
These revolutionaries are not famous – in fact, they're just
like you and me. The one thing they have in common that

gives them the right to wear the revolutionary title: an intense commitment to a cause. This commitment to a cause is also the cornerstone of becoming a Radically Canadian revolutionary.

What is a cause? A cause is nothing more than something you care about deeply. A cause is not a complicated thing. It's so simple, so basic, and so accessible to each one of us that there's absolutely no reason why we all shouldn't have one. All you have to do is find something that's important to you. That something can be as simple as trying to get an ad spot with no money or as revolutionary as creating FedEx. It could even be as big as making your country a better place to live for future generations.

To effectively pursue a cause, you have to break — or at least bend — a few rules. Only by doing this will you create real change, which is something that's often hard to define. According to Richard Farson's *Management of the Absurd,* we all think we want change, but what we really want is more of what we already have. People with money want more money. Athletes want to be more athletic. Smart people want to be smarter, and good-looking people want to be better looking. But having more of what we already have isn't real change. Identifying what we don't have and striving to achieve it is what real change is all about.

The CFL — and, I believe, Canada as well — needs radical change to survive and thrive. Real change is created by ideas that test the rules. Creating real change doesn't come naturally for everyone; people are often more comfortable with slow, manageable change than with dramatic, in-your-face change. Some people are able to embrace change much more easily than others. Similarly, some people are much more willing to take risks. The major difference between those who can and those who can't is the way they deal with failure and rejection.

Being committed to a cause gives you a greater sense of focus and stiffens your resolve. This is one big reason why a true revolutionary is able to ignore or disregard negative emotions and move forward. The other is the knowledge that failure and rejection are not inherently negative. Revolutionaries view setbacks as badges of courage rather than stains of shame. The CFL tried U.S. expansion and from that learned what was wrong with the attempt. The truth is that very few significant accomplishments are ever achieved on the first try. But the first attempt is a great way to test the field, get feedback, and try again, learning continually and adapting to get it right.

There are lots of examples of people who have let minor setbacks get the best of them and as a result abandoned their quests far too soon. Someone once said that the emotions associated with failure or rejection are impossible to experience in a vacuum. In other words, it takes other people to make you feel these emotions — other people who have absolutely no right to determine for you what is right and wrong. You are the only one who can do that. Once you understand this, it gets a lot easier to ignore the narrow-minded views of others and follow your own definition of success. True revolutionaries turn negative emotions – which are often the result of others' insecurities or prejudices – into sources of energy that feed their drive to succeed.

Once you recognize that you are the only one who can determine whether you have truly failed, you will see that there are only two situations in which you can legitimately allow yourself to feel that you have failed. The first is when you don't achieve your goal because you didn't give it 100 percent of your attention and effort. The second is when you set a goal and don't succeed because of a mistake that you've made before. It is impossible to truly fail if you give it everything you have and learn from past mistakes. If the outcome is less than favourable, then the results are simply feedback that you can use to get it right the next time you try. To be a Radical Canadian, you have to be prepared to take risks and accept setbacks.

In the workplace, I have often encountered resistance to new ideas or new ways of doing things. It's natural for people to fear and resist change, particularly if it's a change that they don't understand. They will also resist change that affects them personally, especially if they view it as a threat or if it will affect their routine. We are all creatures of habit, and there is nothing we hate more than people who force us to change our routine. The key to implementing change is education. Explaining to people why change is needed and what it means to them is vital to getting change to stick. All change will be met by some degree of resistance. True revolutionaries know that if they meet with resistance, they are on the right track.

Another source of resistance and negativity is based not on fear or ignorance but rather on jealousy. In the workplace, this is often referred to as the "not my idea" syndrome. There are people in most organizations who believe that they have an exclusive claim on new ideas. Any idea that's not theirs is either a bad idea — no matter how good it is — or it becomes their idea through manipulation. True revolutionaries expect this type of resistance and adjust accordingly by looking for other outlets for their ideas.

During my six years with the CFL, I was constantly confronted with negativity and resistance. This made implementing change more difficult and slowed it down, but it didn't stop change from happening. I knew we were on the right track when we met with resistance; that meant something might change.

The hardest emotion of all to overcome is apathy. This is like trying to generate a good argument with a person who has no opinions. It's next to impossible. The secret to overcoming apathy and getting people stirred up is to find their hot buttons. People are more likely to take action to protect themselves or to avoid something than to achieve something. For example, people will do whatever it takes to avoid being embarrassed or rejected, but they are much less likely to make the same effort to achieve something positive. Herein lies the key to overcoming apathy and winning people over to your side: let people see what will happen if they don't take action, as well as what will happen if they do. Let them sense what it means to them personally and make them feel as though they have something to lose.

Also essential to the cause is a commitment to lifelong learning. Your own failures are great learning experiences, but so are the failures and successes of others. Learn from their experiences, too. It's foolish not to consider the things learned by others. History has a lot to teach us. Becoming a student of the past can give you a head start and can help you avoid the pitfalls that have trapped others. It's one thing to blaze a new trail where no alternative exists, but to start from scratch, if a trail has already been marked out by others, makes no sense at all. No matter what cause you select, chances are that someone else has gone down a similar path. Being a revolutionary does not mean being a loner.

I continue to believe that it is possible to transform organizations the same way we can transform ourselves. Truly successful organizations all demonstrate the same revolutionary traits. They are committed to a cause, they take risks, they break rules, and they learn from their mistakes and forge on. Recognizing this, every business should take a good hard look at its situation and assess whether it has the right environment to nurture revolutionaries.

9

Journey to the Edge of the Abyss, Stage Two

Regrouping from the U.S. venture, the league held its first meeting without any U.S. representation in late February 1996. At first it was strange. But while we missed our former U.S. partners, the new, leaner CFL was a welcome change. We had spent so much time and energy focusing on the problems in the United States that we had neglected the heart and soul of our business: the Canadian teams. What we didn't appreciate at the time was just how much things had deteriorated. As I've mentioned, the Canadian business was in a very weak state even before the U.S. expansion. Our current problems were nothing more than evidence that defensive change is not real change. To be effective, change must be properly focused and directed and, most importantly, it must have progressive meaning that enhances and strengthens an enterprise.

Although expanding to the United States appeared to be

a bold, aggressive move, in reality it was merely defensive – and bound to fail, because it ignored the business's core problems. The fact that the execution was flawed only compounded the existing difficulties. Looking back, it was obvious that most of the CFL's problems were internal and the solutions were all within our control. Unfortunately, rather than dealing with these internal issues head-on, the league consciously ignored them and expanded, providing short-term financial relief while failing to solve the business's inherent problems. This was equivalent to declaring war in a foreign country to hide problems at home. As a result, the league suffered through its U.S. adventure while things back on the home front continued to go downhill, eventually developing into a major crisis. We hadn't taken note of the difference between a defensive reaction and a progressive strategy. Implementing change to avoid problems or cover up other issues isn't real change, any more than wanting more of what we already have is. Defensive change is about surviving, while progressive, real change is pure offence – and success.

Despite all the debris around us, the league still didn't seem to feel any sense of urgency. An outside observer would have assumed from the nature of our discussions in the early part of 1996 that everything was just fine with the good ship CFL. Sure, there was a fleeting remark about some short-term financial challenges with the Ottawa club, but that was about it. Looking back, I know that everyone was well aware of just how bad things were, but a sense of denial persisted. Over time, I started to refer to this style of management as the "if in doubt, punt" approach.

We all knew that our first big problem was likely to come out of Calgary. Larry Ryckman had sent out enough warning signals over the past year so that everyone knew it was just a matter of time before he hit the wall. At the governors' meeting held on March 5, the commissioner informed the group that Ryckman's operating company, Ryckman Financial Corporation, had been put into receivership by the Alberta Treasury Branch (ATB). The receiver's mandate was to oversee the orderly termination of the affairs of the company and its subsidiaries, which included the Calgary Stampeders Football Club.

The CFL's constitution had a provision to deal with a situation like this. It allowed the league to take back the franchise and sell it without any challenges from creditors or the previous owner. This meant that neither the receiver-the ATB-nor any other creditor had the right to seize and sell the franchise. Provided they had the proper security, the creditors could seize the football equipment and the office equipment, but they had no authority to sell the right to play football in the CFL. This provision, combined with the CFL's right to approve all sales, meant that, in theory, the league alone decided who could own a team and under what conditions. But nothing is ever as clear as it seems in the CFL; this right was about to be challenged.

It turns out that the constitution could not protect intellectual property, which, in effect, means that the name and logos of the team might not be protected from creditors if they had been pledged as security. In this situation, the name "Calgary Stampeders" and the white horse logo were the property of the receiver, as was all the football equipment. It was inconceivable that anyone would buy the right to play football in Calgary without using the Stampeders name, which meant that we had to work closely with the receiver to co-ordinate the assets and find a new owner. Fortunately, the receiver was very accommodating and we developeded a good collaborative relationship. However, the situation was further complicated by the fact that the club had already sold and collected over $800,000 worth of season tickets for the upcoming year – money long gone for games that might not be played. This meant that a new owner would have to honour these tickets or risk upsetting thousands of people by asking them to pay for the same ticket twice.

Larry Smith and I were dispatched to Calgary to work with the receiver and find a new owner. Early in the process, the receiver decided that having Ryckman Financial petitioned into bankruptcy, the next step beyond receivership, would help it sort through the complicated financial issues more efficiently. This meant that all deals to sell the company's assets, including the Stampeders, would now have to be approved by the courts. The bankruptcy pro-

ceedings were held in a Calgary courthouse packed with
members of the media, as well as many interested onlook-
ers, most of whom came expressly to catch a glimpse of
Larry Ryckman as his empire came tumbling down.

To his credit, Ryckman attended the proceedings and put
on a very brave face. That night he invited Larry Smith and
me to have dinner with him at one his favourite Italian
restaurants. When we arrived, he was already seated at a
corner table in a large private room, with his back to the
wall. All things considered, I thought he was handling the
stressful situation extremely well. The evening progressed,
and after a few drinks he started to talk about the book he
was going to write, which, according to him, would set the
record straight. Ryckman told Larry Smith that he would
be mentioned in the book and that it would be very complimentary. He then turned to me and said that I, too, would
be mentioned in his book. Without skipping a beat, he
added, "I never did like you." I assumed that meant my part
wouldn't be as complimentary as Larry's. To the best of my
knowledge, he never did write that book.

We were fortunate to find a buyer for the Calgary franchise in Sig Gutsche, who worked with us through all the
red tape of the bankruptcy to buy the Stampeders. He
agreed to honour the season ticket sales, pay the receiver for
the name and equipment, and pay the CFL a modest sum, all
for the right to join a league with an uncertain future.
Without Sig, I'm not sure where we would be today. He

stepped up when no one else would and ensured that the team would continue its long tradition of great football in Calgary. To his credit, he recognized that the club's major asset was its management team and worked hard to keep them together. In the end, his strategy and entrepreneurial risk worked out extremely well for both him and the CFL. Under Sig's leadership, the Calgary club has become one of the most successful franchises in the league.

After Sig's offer to purchase the Calgary club was approved by the board, a feeling of calm washed in. Securing a new owner in Calgary just months before the season was to begin meant that the league was off the hook. You could almost hear the collective sigh of relief. But, as is usually the case, this was just the calm before the storm.

The owner of the B.C. Lions, who had earlier hinted that he wanted to sell the club, informed the league that he had made a deal. This in itself wouldn't have been too upsetting. What *was* upsetting was to whom he was selling. The new owners would be a partnership headed by Nelson Skalbania, a previous CFL owner and a man with a very questionable financial record. There was a sense of disbelief among the governors. Everyone wanted to know, Why Skalbania and why now? The next most asked question was, Can he do this?

Between this announcement and the next board meeting, various board members talked to the current B.C. owner and attempted to convince him to reconsider. He didn't. At the next board meeting, which was held in April in Hamilton, the B.C. Lions club was represented not by Skalbania (or anyone else in the partnership), but by a man who was a complete stranger to everyone in the room. This man was going to be the president and CEO of the club. No one was sure how he had become involved and, to be honest, I'm not sure he even knew. Most of us suspected that he was Skalbania's reluctant front man. The new president explained that he was attempting to put together a partnership of 10 people, who would each own 10 percent of the club. One of these partners was to be Skalbania. Despite a great deal of probing by the governors to try to flush out the names of the other potential partners, the president was unable or unwilling to give any names. The only thing he would say was that the partners would be in place and announced to the public very shortly. Based on that very loose commitment from this total stranger, the league awarded the partnership a conditional franchise. One of the conditions was obviously that he find partners for the partnership. The board asked that this be accomplished by the next meeting.

The entire experience surrounding the ownership of the B.C. club was almost surreal: two months from the start of training camp, with a team that had no ownership, listening to a man that we had never met, who was outlining a plan that, in my opinion, he obviously wanted no part of. To make matters worse, we had no choice but to hope he was successful. It was obvious to me that the league had lost complete control. We couldn't enforce the rules of the league, nor could we control to whom our franchises were sold. We were so helpless that we entrusted the future of the B.C. franchise to a complete stranger — because we had no other alternative. We had punted so often when faced with adversity that we no longer knew how to play the ball.

10

Is There a Limit to How Many Times One Team Can Punt?

As it turned out, the B.C. club didn't meet the deadline for finding partners. Nevertheless, the league allowed the club to begin the 1996 season under Nelson Skalbania's direction. The president who we had met at the last board meeting was long gone and was never to be heard from again.

Soon we were well into the 1996 season and it was clear that Skalbania had yet to find any partners. In fact, he indicated that there were no prospects on the horizon. Skalbania tried to blame the state of the league for his lack of success and, to be fair, this probably had a lot to do with it. The league urged him to continue his efforts. To the best of my knowledge, there was no plan in place if he failed, and no one at the league was asked to develop one.

As if this wasn't enough to make a grown man cry, the board was also told early in 1996 that the situation with the Ottawa franchise was deteriorating further. Season ticket and sponsorship sales were going very poorly. In the words of the club's president, "The sponsors and the fans are fed up." Sometime in July, the board asked that the CFL office prepare a report on the club's position. This responsibility fell on my shoulders. I knew from the beginning that this report was going to be a political time bomb. Inevitably, it was going to upset people – more than likely, many people.

A number of people in the league had a vested interest in what the report said, and I knew that no matter what the results were, they wouldn't be happy. Other people simply refused to acknowledge the severity of the problem. If the report contradicted their views, they wouldn't be happy either. All I could think was "Please don't shoot the messenger." However hard I might try to placate people, I'd be the one who had brought the bad news. I knew that I would probably need a flak jacket for this one.

My review indicated that in the worst case, the Ottawa club was going to need many millions of dollars to complete the year; and if everything went well (which was very unlikely), just slightly less than many millions. I also reported that the entire amount would probably have to be funded by the league, as owner Horn Chen was reluctant to provide more money. I submitted my findings, much to the chagrin of many. As I had expected there was a sense of "That just can't be." Those closest to the situation believed that they could come up with a much better plan and were confident that Chen would step up and help finance the losses. Some were trying to play down the severity of my report by painting a picture of hope.

As a short-term solution, the league agreed to help by lending the club money, on the condition that Chen matched the league's contribution. I knew at the time that the chances of Chen fulfilling his part of the bargain were not good. Meanwhile, Larry Smith was given the challenge of finding a long-term solution.

To cap off a truly memorable July, the Montreal ownership reported that its club was going to incur heavy losses. By this time everyone seemed numb with shock from all the news. Where there should have been panic, there was only denial. On a personal level, I was overwhelmed by the number of problems and their magnitude. I knew I wasn't in this alone, but nevertheless I felt very isolated. For whatever reason, I sensed that I was the only one who comprehended the severity of the situation.

As the summer advanced, things slowly got worse. Despite many new initiatives and a lot of hard work in Ottawa, the club's financial position continued to decline. Meanwhile in B.C., Nelson Skalbania managed to raise some funds, but it was only a drop in the bucket compared to what was really needed. Skalbania warned us that the money was going to run out by the end of August if something wasn't done.

In spite of all this doom and gloom, the strength of the league, the game, and its players continued to thrill the fans. One other positive development was the success of the Radically Canadian campaign. After the beating we took on the U.S. expansion, it seems – to echo Don Cherry – that we had at least limped back to the bench on our own steam. The slogans and the message hit a nerve; at the games there were hundreds of people wearing the "One great game for one great country" or the "Our balls are bigger" T-shirts. While sitting in the stands during a game in Ottawa, I over-heard a group of university students talking about the campaign. One kid said to his friend, "Whoever thought up that Radically Canadian thing should get a raise." It was probably one of the few times during the entire year that I managed a smile.

As the month of August progressed, we started to get the feeling that the house of cards was about to collapse. Every Monday after a weekend of games we would wait and pray that the phone didn't ring, because if it did, it was probably one of the three problem teams warning us that it might not have enough money to pay the players. CFL players don't get paid on a weekly or monthly basis – they are paid after every game. For the average team, this means having to come up with about $150,000 to cover the payroll, including taxes, and other benefits within 24 hours after each game. When a team is struggling, this is a lot of money. If we got to Tuesday without any calls, we would rejoice and check off another week. No news was good news.

By late August, I was fairly certain that my earlier

prediction had been correct and that it would cost millions of dollars to complete the season in Ottawa. Despite rumours to the contrary, Horn Chen was not providing any money. It was clear that the league was going to be on the hook for the full amount.

I had estimated that the CFL office was going to make a profit of about $4 million. In addition to the problem in Ottawa, I warned the board that there were other holes developing with both the B.C. and Montreal teams. I had a responsibility to make sure that everyone understood the severity of the situation: the league could go under if those holes got too deep.

One of those potential problems, the B.C. Lions, was now represented not by Nelson Skalbania but by Mike McCarthy, who was running the club pretty much on his own for Skalbania. Mike's involvement was a welcome change because he provided us with timely information. Mike confirmed what I had suspected all along: the B.C. club had received virtually no funds from the partnership. The club was surviving solely on its meagre ticket sales and the advances from sympathetic sponsors and radio rights holders.

Then we heard from the Montreal franchise. When the club had received permission to move from Baltimore to Montreal, the primary owner had committed to funding the club to a specified level, which we all believed would be enough to see the team through its first season. Even though he had yet to reach that funding level, the owner informed the board that he was reluctant to provide any more money. The estimate at the time was that it was going to take about $1 million or more to complete the season.

Although the league was financially assisting both Ottawa and Montreal during this time, it was not providing any such help to B.C. The CFL's approach to the B.C. situation could best be described as the vulture strategy. The league would simply circle above until the team missed a significant payment — such as a player payroll — and then swoop in. Why take such a position? Because if, for example, a club were to become insolvent and declare bankruptcy, leaving creditors, including the players, unpaid, the league would be legally responsible to only the players. (The league's responsibility for a club's inability to pay its players is set out in the collective bargaining agreement with the players' association.) All the other creditors would be the responsibility of the owner. And unlike the owners of the other two problem teams, Nelson Skalbania had put very little real money into his team, and so the league had little sympathy for his situation. The league simply sat back and waited for the club to miss its first payroll, which would give us the leverage we needed to revoke the franchise.

We didn't have to wait long. One Monday in early September, we got a call from Mike McCarthy, saying that the club didn't have enough money to pay the players for the past weekend's game. We had to wait until a 48-hour period had expired before we could begin the revocation process. I immediately booked a flight to Vancouver.

On Wednesday, I flew out with our insolvency lawyer, Mario Forté, who by then had become one of my closest business associates. The flight was fairly relaxed. Half jokingly, I mentioned that we might be greeted by reporters and cameras when we arrived at the airport. Sure enough, as we descended the escalator and entered the luggage area, the camera lights all came on and I found myself in the middle of a media scrum. Everyone wanted to know if I had the cheques to pay the players and what were we going to tell Skalbania. We managed to escape the hordes and head downtown to begin the legal huddle.

We were in a difficult position, since we couldn't pay the players until Nelson Skalbania gave up the team – and Skalbania didn't want to give up the team. If we were to pay the players before taking legal control, then Skalbania could have thanked us for the money, walked away, and continued operating the team until he missed the next payroll. This was the worst-case scenario. We had to end this nightmare for everybody's sake – and we had to end it now. Further complicating the issue, we also had to wrestle certain rights away from the previous owner, rights that would revert to him in the event of default by Skalbania. We were dealing with three different sets of lawyers. The media were all over the place, and we knew that the players were getting more upset with each passing hour. Many players desperately needed the money to pay their rent or make their car payments. The pressure was unbelievable.

After a full day of negotiations, we finally reached an agreement late in the evening. Skalbania consented to the appointment of a receiver who would take control of the operation and allow the league to step in and pay the players. As Mario Forté and I were walking back to the hotel, Mario admitted that this was one of the most stressful days he had ever experienced. For an insolvency lawyer, this was quite an admission. I felt the same way. I was also struggling to remain calm about what I still had to do: talk to the angry football players who had not yet been paid.

The following day I went out to the training complex and addressed the B.C. Lions. I was in the middle of a large locker room, surrounded by more than 40 large, furious men. I don't really remember what I said, apart from repeating many times that they would be paid immediately and that they wouldn't miss any more paycheques. By the end of that short speech, my shirt was soaked with sweat. After a brief media conference at which I explained the events of the past few days and the next steps, I jumped on a plane and headed home, leaving the B.C. club in the hands of Mike McCarthy. The players got paid the next day.

11

The Ottawa Money Pit

Having just emerged from one fire, we now had to turn our attention to another. The situation in Ottawa had become critical. From the start, it had been sensitive, because the CFL couldn't legally run the team – we could only advise it. Horn Chen was still technically the owner and was ultimately responsible for all the debts and liabilities of the team, of which there were many. This would have been fine, except that he had, for all intents and purposes, abandoned the franchise very early in the season. The league had no option but to lend the club money to keep operating. This arrangement protected us from any creditors who might try to come after the league, rather than Chen, for past or future debts.

The league constantly pushed the boundary between advising and running the Ottawa club. We persuaded Chen to make some management changes. We got so involved that at one point I was signing all the payroll cheques. That didn't last long, though; we were soon called down to Revenue Canada's offices to discuss the state of the club's deductions account. The club owed almost $300,000 in source deductions from the players' salaries, for taxes and Canada Pension Plan payments. We were well aware of the debt, but it wasn't a high priority for us at the time. It was also our mistaken belief that Horn Chen would ultimately be responsible for these liabilities. If we couldn't get money out of him, maybe Revenue Canada could.

During our meeting with Revenue Canada, the tax authorities got a little upset with the club and tempers flared. At one point, the Revenue Canada guy said that if Horn Chen or the club didn't pay the deductions, then they would go after the person who had signed the cheques. Upon hearing those words, I immediately called for a break. Out in the hallway I asked Mario Forté, the insolvency lawyer who had also accompanied me to Vancouver, if they could do that. He said they could. Since it was my name on those cheques, I decided then and there that we would pay the full debt within 24 hours. From that point on, I didn't sign another thing in Ottawa.

That, however, was not the end of our jousting with Revenue Canada. After that meeting, Revenue Canada made arrangements with the Ottawa club for payment within one week after each payroll. As finances started to get tight at the league level, due to the demands of both the B.C. Lions and the Montreal club, we loaned the Ottawa club (through Chen) only enough money to cover the net payroll. If Chen couldn't come up with the money to make the tax remittances, that was his problem – not ours. Now that we were out of the picture, we knew that Chen was on the hook for sure.

Things started to get even tenser toward the end of August – both for the Ottawa team and for the league. The club's tax debt was growing, and Chen had not made any payments. We were concerned that Revenue Canada was going to seize the club's bank accounts and secure future club receivables. That would present a real problem, because the team had negotiated a $200,000 sponsorship with the federal government and the payment was due to be made soon. They had to have an account in which to deposit that money, and if the payment came in after Revenue Canada had seized the account and the receivables, Revenue Canada would take all the money and apply it to its account. We, on the other hand, wanted the money to be used to pay the players. On behalf of the team I started calling everyone I could think of in the federal government, to see if the payment could be expedited. I became a real pest and probably said a few things that I shouldn't have said to some very important people in very high positions. The club eventually got the money – weeks before it was due to be received. Two days after the money was deposited, Revenue Canada seized the account. At the time there was less than $20,000 in the account, which meant that over $180,000 in paycheques had successfully cleared the account and was in the players' hands.

On September 9, 1996, we conducted a conference call with all the governors regarding the fate of the Ottawa club. As best as I could, I outlined the overall financial picture and our various options. In advance of the meeting, I had prepared and distributed a cash-flow projection for Ottawa, which painted a very bleak picture. Immediately, the president of the club challenged the figures, saying that they were too negative and would persuade the board to make the wrong decision. In his opinion, the only possible decision was to keep the team going. He stressed that this was more than an accounting decision, which is an easy thing to say for someone who isn't financially responsible for the consequences of that decision. He tried to present a much more optimistic financial picture than the one I had described. Even over the phone lines, you could sense the friction between us. What he didn't understand was that I wasn't necessarily in favour of shutting down the club. I just wanted to make sure that everyone thoroughly understood the ramifications of whatever decision we were about to make. In my heart, I didn't want to shut down the Ottawa club, but my head was saying otherwise.

In the end, the board decided to continue funding the Ottawa team for the rest of the year. When we hung up the phone, those of us in the league office sat for a couple of minutes in stunned silence. It wasn't that I disagreed with the decision, but I was concerned with the board's apparent inability to comprehend the magnitude of what we had just done. Together we had just made a decision that would put the future of the CFL in real jeopardy, yet no one seemed to be too upset. What was I missing?

12

Balancing the Grey Cup

Our next face-to-face board meeting was September 27,
1996 – my birthday. I reported that the league was still on
track to make $4 million, but it was going to cost many
millions of dollars more than that to fund the three problem clubs for the balance of the season. That meant we
would have a major deficit. The question was, Where was
this money going to come from?

As usual when I presented financial projections, there
were some people who just couldn't accept how bad the
financial situation was and would jump all over my projections. This had become a recurring event. It certainly would
have been easier for me to take an optimistic view, but I was
the one who was going to have to live with the consequences
if the optimistic projections didn't come true. The stress was
making me crazy.

It was around this time that Larry Smith announced that

the league office was taking a 5 percent pay cut. Larry
believed that this would send a message to the players' association that we were prepared to make sacrifices and that
they should be, too. At one point Larry even wrote to the
players explaining the seriousness of the situation, much to
the chagrin of the players' association. I'm not sure if the
pay cut sent out the right message or not, but what I do
know is that it really upset our staff. Forcing a junior person
making $20,000 a year to take a pay cut that might save
$1,000 over a one-year period wasn't going to accomplish
much, other than forcing the person to look for a new job.
The amount saved by the pay cut was more than offset by
a decline in morale. To make matters worse, Larry then
conducted a media conference to announce the decision.
The problem was that, although a pay cut had been discussed, not all the staff had been advised about it. My own
family found out about the pay cut when it was announced
on the radio.

It was also reported around this time that the 1996
Hamilton Grey Cup had sold about 25,000 tickets to date.
What we didn't report was that ticket sales had come to a
screeching halt. This was a concern for the league for two
reasons. First of all, the league desperately needed the money from this game, since the guarantee from the region of
Hamilton was a major part of the league's projected $4 mil-
lion profit in 1996. Even though we had a signed contract,
there were sufficient extenuating circumstances to justify a

reduction in the fee if the region wanted to pursue it. They could have argued, quite fairly, that all the negative press about the state of the league was affecting their ticket sales and that a reduction in the contract was warranted.

The lack of ticket sales, combined with a lukewarm response from corporate Hamilton, was also a problem because the Grey Cup organizing committee didn't have enough money to cover its own expenses and was forced to go back and ask for more money from the city. This created a very tense political environment and was the source of some friction between the league, the city, and the organizing committee.

All this friction made what I had to do next very difficult. All my financial projections – the subject of constant criticism – had come true. The league desperately needed an advance on the rights fee from the Grey Cup committee so that we could pay our bills. In light of the tension that existed between the parties, this was a difficult thing to ask. I also didn't think that it was wise to borrow from the future to pay for the debts of the past. Although the committee agreed to the advance – essentially saving the league – I still had to walk a very fine line. We needed money to pay our bills and pay the players in Ottawa, B.C., and Montreal, but I also had to make sure we had enough left to pay the players for the Grey Cup. For the league, the total cost to stage the Grey Cup is about $1.5 million, of which about $800,000 is the player payroll. My greatest fear was that we would play the game and not have enough money to pay the players. This would have been a huge embarrassment both for the league and for me personally. I couldn't let that happen.

For the next two months, my life was basically cash-flow management and disaster planning. I wasn't thinking past November 26, 1996 — the Grey Cup game. My only concern was that we got through the playoffs, played the Grey Cup game, and paid the players. I would do whatever I could — within legal limits — to make that happen. This goal justified our actions in Ottawa with Revenue Canada, the desperate manoeuvres taken to get the $200,000 federal sponsorship in the bank, and various other actions. This period was unbelievably stressful.

The closer we got to the Grey Cup game, the more tense things became. The situation in Ottawa continued to deteriorate, and our relationship with the Montreal owner worsened. This owner had been a reluctant partner throughout the 1996 season, but we worked hard to maintain a cordial relationship with him. The league was sending money to Montreal on a weekly basis, but not nearly as much as what went to Ottawa and B.C. The owner put some money into the club during this time, but it was nowhere near what was needed. Nevertheless, we swallowed our pride and kept working with him — not because we thought he would be around in 1997, but because every dollar we could get out of him saved the league a dollar and brought us one step closer to the Grey Cup game.

By the time the week of the 1996 Grey Cup arrived, ticket sales were still very poor. The stadium seating had been augmented with temporary stands, which brought the total seating up to 45,000. But on the Monday before the Sunday game, only 27,000 seats had been sold. Still, there was a chance that sales would pick up after the Argonauts' win in the eastern division final the previous day. Since Toronto is only an hour down the road from Hamilton, we hoped that many people would buy tickets now that their team was in the game. We waited with bated breath to see how Monday's sales went in Toronto. Unfortunately, the response was less than overwhelming. Something had to be done; we couldn't afford to have 18,000 empty seats at what the media were hyping as the last Grey Cup game.

Geoff Fardy, the CFL's vice president of marketing, hatched a plan to work with the Tim Hortons coffee chain, a CFL partner, to sell discounted tickets at their outlets in the Hamilton area. Unfortunately, the details of the plan were leaked to the media, who threw it back in our face as evidence that the CFL was indeed on its last legs. Naturally, all the naysayers, the ones who couldn't come up with a better idea, agreed with the media's position and jumped all over us. We took the criticism in stride, and it turned out to be the right thing to do. Our plan sold about 10,000 tickets, filling seats that otherwise would have been empty.

At the board meeting the day before the game, I reviewed the league's financial position. As strongly as I could, I emphasized the fact that the CFL was in severe financial distress. The league's current liabilities exceeded its current assets by many millions of dollars. I also stressed the point that, because of the league's structure, each club and possibly each governor might be individually and collectively liable if the league was unable to pay its bills. This went over like a lead balloon.

Game day started out well. The game was scheduled to begin at 6:00 pm, and by noon the stadium was ready to go. The commissioner's luncheon went off without a hitch. But as we emerged from the windowless room around 2:00 pm, we noticed that snowflakes were starting to fall. Within an hour, it was a full-fledged snowstorm. By the time the fans were begining to arrive, the wet snow was coming down hard. The field and the seats were completely covered. Our sponsors were beside themselves. They had paid millions of dollars for signs both on and beside the field, which were now almost impossible to see.

Yet the game got played, and it turned out to be one of the most exciting and most watched games of all time. The final attendance was around 37,000, which was respectable but still disappointing. Indeed, we were saved by the fact that it had snowed. Everyone watching on TV was so taken by the snow-covered field and the adverse conditions that the number of people in the stands was secondary to the excitement of the game. It was appropriate that the season from hell should end this way. No matter how badly we screwed up the business of the game, no matter what the environmental conditions, the game continued to shine through all the chaos.

I watched the game with my family from my seat in the stands and tried to keep warm and dry, which proved to be impossible. I wasn't interested in attending any pre-game functions nor was I interested in sitting with any of the many dignitaries up in the dry private boxes. The year had been very difficult, and I was so exhausted that all I wanted to do was watch the game in relative quiet. After the game, our family jumped in the car and headed home, avoiding any post-game celebrations. I was proud of the fact that the game got played under very difficult conditions – environmentally, financially, and politically – but I was in no mood to celebrate. I knew that most of our problems were still ahead of us.

A number of pundits have suggested that eventually all organizations will change, whether they want to or not. If they can't do it on their own, then change will be forced on them by a calamity. There is no doubt that our look into the abyss in 1996 was a full-blown disaster for the CFL. We had no choice but to change the way we did business quickly, or we would have fallen into the abyss and disappeared forever. I often wonder why it takes a catastrophe to force organizations to change. Based on my experience with the CFL, my words of advice are: Implement real change before it is forced on you.

Looking back, I believe many people thought the CFL was invincible. How could anything ever happen to it? After all, it had been around for hundreds of years, experienced all kinds of abuse at the hands of all kinds of people, and survived. There was this sense that no matter how bad things got, the CFL would always be there. Upon reflection, that was certainly a naive and dangerous belief. It was almost as if the league believed that the game was above the economic realities of other businesses. I wonder if the people who ran Eaton's thought that way as well.

The truth is that the CFL was lucky. Many businesses never get a second chance. The league worked its way out of this mess with the loyalty and understanding of its key partners; the eventual support of the NFL (financial and otherwise); and the commitment and perseverance of many hard-working, dedicated people. The CFL has to learn from its past and start dealing with the reality that it is just another business that has to earn its right to exist, day in and day out. It simply can't be allowed to get anywhere near that abyss again. Contrary to the belief of the naysayers out there, the CFL has a very exciting future ahead of it, provided the business is run in a professional and strategic manner.

From a personal point of view, the 1996 season was a very difficult period. Even though I wasn't responsible for the mess, I felt responsible for the solution. I couldn't imagine telling people that I was part of the last days of the CFL. The sense of responsibility was huge. At one point, right in the middle of the battle, it seemed that there would be no end to the continuous stream of catastrophic problems. To survive, we had to make very difficult decisions. Every move we made came under scrutiny. At every turn we were second-guessed and criticized. It was like living in a toxic fishbowl. Perhaps people would have been a little more sympathetic if they had known how serious the situation was, but we couldn't make it public, for fear of a total meltdown. I certainly learned a lot about the benefits and the challenges of being Canadian, deep in the defensive line of a Canadian business. I also promised myself that whether I was involved in the league or not, it must never be allowed to go through anything like that again. It was time to go on the offensive.

Two weeks after the Hamilton Grey Cup, the board held a special meeting to deal with the many challenges ahead. It was at this meeting that our chairman announced Larry Smith's resignation as commissioner. In response to this development, one of the league's governors was asked to review all matters relating to the governance of the league, including the process for appointing a new commissioner. This would be the beginning of a whole new roller coaster ride for me.

13

The 1997 Season: The Long Road Back

The first three months of 1997 continued to be all about survival. The cash-flow situation — or, more accurately, the lack of cash — made the planning and preparation for the new season rather interesting, to say the least. Over the years, we had gotten pretty good at stretching a penny, but this situation presented an even greater challenge. What money we could scrape together was used almost exclusively to pay our salaries and keep the lights on, which left very little for debt reduction. I was surprised by how understanding and co-operative our many creditors were. Despite our financial problems and the persistent rumours of the CFL's demise, our partners stood by us and never questioned our good intentions. I'm very proud of the fact that most of them were still partners years later.

Apart from cash management, our major focus was sponsorship sales. Given the uncertain environment and the results of the previous year, the dollars weren't exactly flowing in. One of the primary benefits for a corporate sponsor is the positive association of its product or service with an organization that people admire and respect. Needless to say, the CFL didn't deliver on that benefit in 1996. As if that wasn't enough, we also failed to deliver on the secondary benefit: straight advertising exposure. The snow-covered field in Hamilton had smothered every sign in the stadium, giving viewers the impression that we had no sponsors at all. It's easy to understand why we were greeted with skeptical sighs when we showed up on our sponsors' doorsteps looking for support again in 1997. Thankfully, our long-term supporters didn't have the heart to turn us down — more out of pity than anything else. This same emotion, however, didn't work at all when it came to attracting new sponsors. Pity is not a great selling tool.

We were also in the uncomfortable position of not having a location for the 1997 Grey Cup. Montreal was scheduled to stage the game, but the team was put into bankruptcy at the end of 1996. A new owner was found, but understandably he had no desire to take on a commitment of this magnitude, which left us without a place to play our biggest and most profitable game of the year. The only team in the league that was capable of stepping up and making the game a success in such a short period of time was the Edmonton Eskimos. Fortunately, the club agreed to step in — a huge risk that was very much appreciated by everyone. This was the first of many actions taken by individual clubs that marked the beginning of a new period of partnership and co-operation among league members.

On the downside, however, in early 1997 the league decided to suspend the Ottawa franchise. It was obvious that Horn Chen would not be back, and there didn't seem to be any white knights on the horizon. From a business perspective, it was a very easy decision, but emotionally it was very difficult. Ottawa had been in the league right from the start, and professional football had been played there for over 100 years. It was hard to believe that there wouldn't be a team in our nation's capital. The decision was particularly difficult for me personally, because Ottawa was where I had first become a fan. I took the loss of the club very hard.

In the interest of survival, the CFL held talks with the NFL throughout the entire winter and early spring of 1997 about a strategic alliance. The NFL agreed to lend the CFL US$3 million, to be paid back over time, to help us regroup from the 1996 season. In addition to this short-term financial assistance, they would also provide long-term marketing help. On April 11, we held a media conference to announce the new alliance. Our chairman, John Tory, and the NFL's commissioner, Paul Tagliabue, sat together on a podium in a Toronto ballroom in front of a packed room and announced what turned out to be one of the most significant developments in the history of the CFL. If you listened carefully, you could almost hear the momentum swing in the CFL's direction. A sense of optimism enveloped the room. The alliance gave the league a new shot at respectability and credibility – a new beginning.

Over the next few months, we met with the NFL on a number of occasions to discuss our marketing challenges and areas where they could help. For most of the NFL representatives, the CFL was a unique challenge. Their experience with the NFL had taught them how to market and maximize their brand, which is definitely one of the strongest in the world, but they had some difficulty wrapping their heads around rebuilding a weak brand. The differences between our two nations made the task even more complex.

We spent hours talking about the things that made Canada unique and the challenges associated with marketing in this massive and diverse country. Many of their solutions involved investing huge amounts of money, which we just didn't have. This seemed to frustrate our NFL colleagues. In the end, we decided to focus our joint efforts on two initiatives. The first was a grassroots program designed to generate new football fans, and the second was a joint sponsorship sales program. The grassroots program was focused on the development of young football fans. We weren't concerned with whether they grew up to be NFL or CFL fans, as long as they learned to appreciate the game of football. This strategy was supported by research that told us that the majority of Canadian football fans supported both leagues.

The Flag Football Canada program, as it was called, had two major thrusts. The first was an extension of a similar program run by the NFL in the United States. The program provided participating schools with curriculum guides, footballs, flags, and T-shirts for participating teachers. With the help of an outside agency, we solicited elementary schools that wanted to participate in the program. In the first year, 1999, we focused on eastern-division cities and then expanded the program to include all of the CFL cities and beyond. Teachers in these schools would follow the curriculum guide and teach the basics of flag football in their physical education classes. By 2000, the program had grown to include over 400 schools across Canada and more than 400,000 kids.

Although we promoted the in-school program together, in reality the NFL did most of the work and paid most of the costs. Without the NFL, the CFL could never have taken on such an aggressive program. It has been very successful and, based on television ratings and attendance, the program has paid real dividends for the CFL. In the end, our goal of generating new football fans worked. Which league they cheered for was irrelevant – what was important was that we were strengthening the game in Canada.

The second part of the program was called "Practise With The Pros." This involved bringing together players from the NFL and the CFL and staging a practice session for kids of various ages. The first one was held in Hamilton and involved players from the Tiger-Cats and the Buffalo Bills, all together on one field, teaching young kids the basics of football. That first session was a great hit and led to many more. In addition to providing a great opportunity to promote the relationship between the CFL and the NFL, these sessions also generated a new group of fans.

Early in our talks with the NFL, I visited their offices in New York. Everyone I met with was very co-operative and helpful. But I was totally overwhelmed by the size and scope of their operation. They occupied more floors than we had employees. When I left, I felt like the poor cousin from the sticks who had come to visit the big city. I was having a hard time relating what they did, to our little football league. The gap between where they were and where we were was huge.

As for the joint sponsorship initiative, it quickly became obvious that it wasn't going to work. Whenever we visited a potential corporate partner and tried to sell them on dual involvement, they looked at us strangely and wondered what we were up to. We came to realize that companies allocated their sponsorship dollars by industry category and that they had only so much to spend on football. Their reaction to our joint approach was either to divide what they had between the two of us or, more likely, to focus on one league only. We might have been slow, but we were not stupid. There was no way we were going to continue leading the competition right into the hands of new sponsors. The NFL realized this as well. We eventually stopped trying to sell together and mutually acknowledged that we were competing for the same sponsors.

This corporate competition was most obvious between our beer partners. During my tenure, the CFL was proudly associated with Molson's, while the NFL has long been associated with Labatt's and Budweiser in Canada. This led to a few awkward situations over the years, the funniest of which occurred at the 1999 Super Bowl in Miami. The NFL had sold the CFL a limited number of tickets for the game and reserved a few rooms in a specific hotel for us. All of the NFL's international friends and sponsors were to be lodged in this hotel, including the people from Labatt's. The problem arose when we decided to invite the Molson representatives as our guests. When we arrived in Miami, we found out that we had been reassigned to a different hotel way out by the airport. It was obvious that the NFL didn't want the Molson people anywhere near their guests from Labatt's, so we were banished to the boonies.

CFL marketing vice president Geoff Fardy and I arrived the day before our Molson guests and checked into our new hotel. Unfortunately, it was located right underneath the approach path to one of the airport runways. As we sat by the pool, we realized that the constant noise from the planes was so loud that talking was next to impossible. On top of that, the hotel was so far from everything that we might as well have been in Orlando. We were quite concerned that our Molson partners would be less than impressed with the accommodations. When we went to bed that night, I sensed that Geoff was agitated – and when he gets like that you never know what he might do.

When I got up the next morning, Geoff was nowhere to be found. By 10:00 am, I still hadn't heard from him and I was getting worried. He finally turned up shortly thereafter and told me to pack, because we were changing hotels. I knew better than to ask too many questions, so I jumped into the rented van with a feeling of apprehension. Geoff had been up and out by 4:00 am, and by 6:00 am he had managed to get us two of the best suites in a hotel on South Beach, which is the place to be in Miami. And the hotel just happened to be owned by Gloria Estefan. He also negotiated his way out of our commitment at the old hotel by selectively bribing a few employees with bottles of wine. When I saw our new accommodations, I was concerned about the price – until I discovered that Geoff had also arranged an incredible deal. The two first-class suites ended up costing us the same as our rooms at the airport strip. When the Molson guys arrived, they were duly impressed. As people back at the NFL hotel found out about our relocation, we were inundated with an endless string of curious and envious visitors. We heard that the NFL person responsible for our excommunication wasn't all that pleased with our little coup.

Although we were able to upgrade our hotel, we couldn't do anything about our seats for the game. We ended up in the second-last row from the top, in the end zone. We didn't take it personally, though, because they put most of their key Canadian partners up there as well. At least we had a great view of the planes on the fly-by.

Over the next few years, our alliance with the NFL focused on the areas where we worked best together, particularly grassroots development. Our mutual objective was and still is the development of new, young football fans. It's hard to evaluate how much the flag program had to do with the increase in the CFL's ratings for the younger demographic group, but I know it played a large role. Despite our initial problems and our fun at the Miami Super Bowl, the NFL's involvement has been an integral part of the CFL's turnaround. Canadians owe the NFL a debt of gratitude for their help in saving the league. In some people's eyes, they may be the big bad Americans, but in my eyes, they were our saviours. Without their help, we would never be where we are today.

With our newfound stability, we set out to stop the bleeding and build for the future. The league reinforced its salary cap and put steps in place to strictly enforce the rules. The teams started to share information that would help them lower their costs and manage the game in a professional and fiscally responsible manner. At the same time, we started to rebuild our revenue base.

Despite our efforts, the league's sponsorship revenue decreased slightly in 1997. We did lose a few sponsors who had become fed up with the way we conducted our business —

and who could blame them? However, we managed to keep most of our sponsors. We accomplished this by making them a very unusual promise. We put a clause in all their contracts in which we basically promised not to embarrass them. If we did, the amount they had to pay was substantially reduced. Even with this promise, many sponsors were reluctant to sign on again. Many stayed because they knew that if they abandoned us, the league might not make it. For whatever reason, many of our key partners stuck with us and, as time would prove, their trust was well placed.

The highlight of the 1997 season (other than the fact that we started and finished the season with the same number of teams) was the Grey Cup game in Edmonton. The stands were packed with over 60,000 people. As the national anthem was sung, all the spectators turned over placards that they had been given, to reveal the largest Canadian flag I've ever seen. Standing on the sidelines as the anthem was sung and the flag was created, I was overwhelmed by emotion.

Any doubts about why I put myself through all the stress and headaches over the past two years disappeared that night. I was so proud to be involved with the CFL and I was extremely proud to be a Canadian. Immediately after the national anthem was the coin toss. I had been selected to flip the coin and I was pumped. As I strode out to centre field, I was overcome by the moment. I was on national television, about to flip the coin to start the 1997 Grey Cup game – the same Grey Cup that I had watched as a kid with my parents. Wow!

I wouldn't say I was nervous, but I was excited. The referee showed the coin to the two captains, explained which side was heads and which was tails, and then gave me the coin. The hand-held CBC camera turned and focused on me in anticipation of the toss. The coin was huge: I panicked. I don't know what I was thinking, but I was expecting a coin the size of a loonie, not a Frisbee. Instead of simply taking it in my hand and throwing it in the air, I tried to put the coin on my thumb and flip it. It was so big that I had a hard time balancing it. It felt like two minutes had passed before I got the coin in a position where I could safely flip it without dropping it, and then I was so concerned that it would fall off my thumb that I didn't toss it very high. After that day, I became a real student of the techniques involved in coin tossing. I watched closely, hoping to learn the finer points, which I managed to put to good use when I again tossed the coin for the 2000 Grey Cup game in Calgary. I'm proud to say that I didn't make the same mistake twice, and the coin was tossed high and confidently. You see, there is something to be learned from past mistakes.

14

Behind the Scenes: Playing Politics

The 1997 season started out relatively calmly and unevent-
fully, but it was to turn into a political skirmish that had
repercussions throughout that year and into the next seasons. In August 1997, I resigned my position in the CFL, but
I subsequently rescinded that notice and stayed on as the
new president of the league. The politics behind this development were unusual, but not compared to the politics to
come in the next years.

I often hear people complain about the politics in their
office and how much they are bothered by them. I've heard
many of these same people say that they have no intention
of playing the game, and if playing politics is what it takes
to get ahead, then advancement is a sacrifice they're prepared to make. The reality is that politics and gamesmanship exist in just about any activity that involves two or
more people. Generally speaking, politics are omnipresent.

Accepting this fact is critical to your success.

Learning the rules of the game is crucial to implementing change. When confronted with many kicks to the head, a team must strategize. To think for one moment that major advancements are possible without fighting through red tape and politics is naive. To really make a difference, you must realize that politics are part of life and then learn effective gamesmanship.

I'm not a natural politician, but over the years I have learned to play the game. I had to learn because it became obvious very early in my career that success in the workplace is based not solely on how well you do your job but also on how well you communicate your successes. When Larry Smith resigned as commissioner of the CFL in late 1996, I was the chief operating officer, reporting to Larry. In this position, I was responsible for all the day-to-day business operations of the league, while Larry focused on the future direction of the business. After Larry left, I assumed many of his responsibilities as they related to business development, while John Tory took the official title of commissioner, in addition to his role as chairman. There was some discussion about looking for a new commissioner, but no one seemed to be in a big hurry to get the search started. I believed that most people thought that together John and I were doing a more than adequate job. Apparently, this was not the case.

During the winter and early spring months of 1997,

there were more discussions about finding a new commissioner and committees were formed, but – despite hints of movement – very little action. On the business side, we were making headway and slowly winning back the respect of the media and the trust of our fans. There was a new sense of stability surrounding the league.

As the year progressed, the search for a new commissioner became public knowledge, but the internal search committee charged with finding a replacement for Larry had made little or no progress. This aggravated me for a couple of reasons. From a business perspective, it created an environment of extended uncertainty. Our partners wanted to know what was going on. The longer we lived with this uncertainty, the harder it was to move the business ahead. I sensed that the search committee didn't seem too interested in having me apply for the position, despite the fact that I was already doing the job and, in my opinion, doing it well. I also had the distinct impression that if I didn't get the job, my position could be in jeopardy.

Toward the end of April 1997, the search for the new commissioner finally kicked into high gear. An advertisement was placed in the *Globe and Mail*, outlining the requirements of the job. I sent in my resumé. Much to the chagrin of the search committee, I'm sure, the firm in charge of the search process gave me an interview. I passed the first phase and was asked to meet with the board's search committee as one of five finalists.

The search committee consisted of three governors. John Tory, the league's chairman and acting commissioner, sat in on the interviews as an observer. I knew that it was going to be an uphill battle, so I decided to prepare a detailed strategic plan for the league, including specific tactics and action plans. One month after my first interview, I finally got an audience with the committee. I thought the presentation went extremely well. In fact, I think they were somewhat shocked, since the plan was so simple and logical that they were left with little to add or criticize. All things being equal, I felt as though I should be their man. The problem was that things were not equal.

About two days later, John Tory called and asked me to his office. I sensed by the tone of his message that the news was not going to be good. John was basically the messenger for the search committee, and he told me that although my interview was perhaps the best, the committee had decided not to proceed with any of the finalists. The committee was, however, going to continue and expand its search. I wasn't given any real reasons why I was being rejected. To add insult to injury, I was told that once a new commissioner was secured, chances were that there wouldn't be a need for both of us. In other words, not only did I not get the job, but I was also being told that my time with the CFL was about to come to an end. I asked if the board concurred with this decision, and the answer was yes.

I was very angry when I left the meeting. I knew that my

chances of winning over the search committee were slim, but I never expected that their decision would be to expand the search and turf me. I was also stunned that the board fully supported this decision. I thought I had some supporters on the board who would stand up for me, but it seemed that I had none. I had pretty much made up my mind to quit right then and there, but I waited to make my decision public until after I had negotiated my exit arrangements. This was done by June 16, 1997, just six days before a scheduled board meeting in Calgary.

Once I had the security of an exit deal, I wrote to John Tory and tendered my resignation, effective October 1, 1997. A media release went out that day as well. As soon as the news became public, I started getting calls from surprised and perplexed governors. It didn't take me long to realize that the board not only didn't support the search committee's decision but, in fact, had been totally unaware of it.

The next morning I got on a plane for Calgary to attend the board meeting. The story of my resignation was all over the newspapers. I had known that the sports media would pick up the story, but I never expected it to receive as much press as it did. I was also surprised by the spin on the story. Most reporters looked at my departure as a huge disadvantage for the league, since it left a void so soon after Larry Smith's departure. Some reporters questioned the entire search process. In relation to my resignation, one governor was quoted as saying, "I'm disappointed, I don't understand it, and I'm awaiting further discussion at the board of governors meeting." Based on my discussions the previous day with a couple of governors and the tone of the media coverage, I knew we were in for a very interesting meeting.

The first item on the agenda in Calgary was governance. In this case, the topic was the search process, my resignation, and the events that led to it. I'm not really sure what was said in the meeting, because I was asked to leave the room, along with the other league staff. After an hour or so, we were called back in and the meeting progressed as though nothing had happened. At the first break, I learned that the search process had been put on hold and that John would speak to me later about an arrangement that the board hoped would convince me to reconsider my decision.

Over the next month or so, John and I negotiated in good faith toward a deal that would keep me on, but our discussions didn't seem to be going anywhere. The league wanted to maintain the status quo, which meant I would continue running the day-to-day business, with the same title, and John would continue to be the chairman and acting commissioner. It should be noted that John was the acting commissioner by default; the CFL's constitution states that if there is no commissioner, the chairman becomes the commissioner until a new one is found. In my opinion, I was fulfilling most of the commissioner's duties, and therefore I wanted the title.

Eventually I gave in and agreed to stay, with the new title of president. I decided to stay because I thought that I could really make a difference and because I wanted to prove to the board, particularly the people on the search committee, that they had made a mistake. I was well aware that my job was going to be much more difficult because of the way the search had ended. But I was prepared for that. I belive that standing up for myself is an important way to combat hostile politics. I think that as long as you're providing a first-class product, you should expect to be treated well, and I give that advice to anybody dealing with a similar situation. You seldom get anything in this world unless you ask for it, so ask for a lot. I fought for what I wanted and got most of what I had asked for.

On August 30, just 19 days after I signed back on, I found out just how difficult my job would be. A reporter stumbled on a major discrepancy when separately interviewing a member of the search committee and John Tory. The governor, Lynn Bishop, told the reporter, "There's a search on for a new commissioner. A new form of leadership is required." Recognizing a controversy, the reporter called John Tory, who, in the reporter's words, was "struck speechless when he heard the criticism." Soon after speaking with John Tory, the reporter got another call from the governor, who said, "I just got a call from a very upset John Tory." Then Lynn Bishop added, "There was a search for a new commissioner, but it's been called off."

Despite all the uncertainty surrounding governance, our efforts to strengthen the league were working. The 1997 Grey Cup was a huge success, thanks primarily to the hard work of the Edmonton organizing committee. We were on the verge of a major breakthrough, and we entered the 1998 season with a renewed sense of optimism.

15

The 1998 Season: Competition Is a Great Thing

We began the 1998 season by preparing for upcoming television negotiations. The existing three-year deal with the CBC, our conventional carrier, was coming to a close, while the contract with TSN, our cable partner, still had two years left to run. Traditionally, the league split its television rights between cable and conventional broadcasters. Conventional, or over-the-air, signals – such as the CBC, CTV, and Global – can be picked up with an antenna. Cable channels – such as TSN, CTV Sportsnet, and MuchMusic – on the other hand, require subscription to a cable service.

At that point, the CBC had carried CFL games for longer than anyone could remember. Back in the league's prime, both the CBC and CTV aired the games, and those who are old enough will remember when both networks carried the Grey Cup game at the same time. CBC announcers would call one half of the game, the CTV team would take over for the other half, and the two crews would work together before the game and at halftime. However, for the last decade or so, the only conventional broadcaster interested in bringing the CFL to Canadians was the CBC. This meant that there was only one party to negotiate with — which meant there were no negotiations. We had to take whatever they offered. This resulted in declining broadcast rights fees (relative to inflation) over this period of time.

All this changed in 1997, when CTV announced the launch of a new national cable sports channel, called CTV Sportsnet, to compete head-on with TSN. This new channel would begin broadcasting in the fall of 1998. This development changed the entire broadcast environment and created some real competition for programming rights.

I started the process of soliciting expressions of interest from all the conventional broadcasters at the end of 1997. Since the league had two years remaining on its cable deal with TSN, my initial approach was to secure a new two-year deal for the conventional rights. If we were successful in obtaining such a deal, then all of the rights would come up for renegotiation at the same time, putting the CFL in a better negotiating position in two years' time. I anticipated a bid from the CBC, but I was hoping that CTV and perhaps Global would join in as well. CTV was our best bet, because they would eventually need cable programming for CTV Sportsnet. If I could convince them that purchasing the conventional rights now would give them an edge when the

cable rights were available in two years, I might get them
to the table. CTV did show significant interest but, to my surprise, so did TSN, which was determined to keep the CFL out
of the hands of CTV. In the end, the league received offers
from the CBC, Global, CTV, and TSN. TSN's decision to bid on
the conventional broadcast rights, although they were only
a cable broadcaster, was a bold and risky move but, as it
turned out, the risk paid off.

Over the next month, I followed up on all the offers and
kept the board apprised of what was happening. After a
lot of gamesmanship and tense negotiating, it was TSN
that came up with the best offer. I recommended that the
board accept the TSN offer, which included both cable and
conventional broadcasting rights. The deal required TSN to
arrange to air at least the Grey Cup and the playoffs on a
conventional broadcaster, which they later did with the CBC.
The five-year deal not only doubled our previous annual
rights revenue but it also provided a multi-million-dollar
signing bonus.

Although the loan from the NFL was critical to the CFL's
survival, the TSN deal was one of the most significant events
in our turnaround. In effect, it was the launching pad for all
that was about to happen. I will always look back at signing
this deal as the turning point for the league – and one of
my personal highlights as well. I still keep a copy of the
cheque for the signing bonus in my daily "To Do" folder,
and a big smile comes across my face every time I look at it.

TSN has turned out to be a valuable partner for the CFL. They invested heavily in production and promotion, and together we increased the ratings by a whopping 80 percent over the next three years, which is almost unheard of in the world of sports programming. This increase took the CFL from a being a good television product to being a great television product. The ratings success contributed significantly to our sponsorship growth, exposed our game to more Canadians, and elevated our overall image, which brought more people to our sidelines.

Announcing the TSN deal created a whole new sense of stability and credibility for the league. On the heels of this deal, the league negotiated a major deal with Adidas to supply the teams with shoes and practice wear. Many more new deals also followed. Our strategy from 1997 was starting to pay dividends: we had promised our sponsors that we wouldn't embarrass them, and we didn't. In fact, we worked very hard at over-delivering on every promise that we made. Geoff Fardy and his marketing team provided our sponsors with a level of service they had never experienced before. The sponsors all returned from the 1997 Grey Cup brimming with pride and excitement, anxious to be involved again in 1998. By the time we got to the 1998 Grey Cup in Winnipeg, the league had more than doubled its sponsorship revenue from the previous year. Once all the dust had settled, we found that the league had made a record profit in 1998. For the first time in years, the CFL

was able to share the profits with its teams, even after making the first payment on the NFL loan and paying off all
the remaining debts from 1996. The total distribution
exceeded $1 million per team that year.

The Grey Cup game in Winnipeg was a tremendous
success for the league. Unfortunately, it wasn't as much of
a success for the organizing committee, as the game didn't
sell out. The city was preoccupied with the upcoming
Pan-American Games, which were to begin just eight
months after the Grey Cup. The people and the businesses
in Manitoba were already under enormous pressure to buy
tickets and provide support for the Pan-Am games. In hindsight, perhaps the city took on a little too much in too short
a period of time. But in light of this extremely competitive
environment and the general strain on the community, I
believe the committee did a great job. They did themselves
and their province proud.

After the game, my wife and I returned to our hotel
room and watched the news. The CTV national news did a
very positive piece on the game. The game had gone right
down to the wire, with a last-minute field goal by Hamilton to beat Calgary. The CTV reporter focused on the game
and the party atmosphere around the game. The whole
piece reflected very well on the league. We then flipped to
the CBC national news and watched their story, which was
just the opposite. The camera spent more time focused on
the section of empty stands than it did on the game. The

tone of the report was basically, "Great game, but where are all the people?" I was furious.

When I got back to the office the next week, I called the CBC's head of sports to get an explanation. He never even tried to apologize. He told me that he couldn't control the news department, and if that's what they wanted to focus on, there wasn't anything he could do about it. We also discussed the pre-game show, in which the CBC had done a piece on all the league's controversial former owners. This report included a phone interview with Bruce McNall, the former Toronto Argonauts owner, showing a picture of the prison where he was serving time for various indiscretions. It was my position that this report made fun of the CFL and was inappropriate for a lead-up to the national championship game. Again, the CBC head of sports responded that it was great entertainment and he didn't see anything wrong with it. I concluded that the network just didn't appreciate the complexities of integrated marketing and the relationship between ratings and positive promotion.

Even so, the best part of 1998 was our television ratings. They were up 26 percent for TSN and 20 percent for the CBC; the Grey Cup game itself was up 10 percent. These figures were beyond anyone's expectations. Our success was the result of hard work and a focus on the basics. My experience in turnarounds has taught me that your chances of winning are much better if your offence is focused on ball control rather than making the big play to score a touchdown.

Although the big plays may win you the occasional game, it's the basic plays, executed well, that ensure consistent long-term success. That's what we did in the CFL. We did a whole lot of little things better, and over time they started to add up.

16

Behind the Scenes: The Politics Get Dirty

Perhaps because things were going so well, John Tory announced in the spring of 1998 that this would be his last year as chairman and acting commissioner. He intended to step down right after the Grey Cup in Winnipeg. In light of this announcement and the effect it might have on me, I reluctantly asked John if he would bring up the topic of governance at the next board meeting, which was to be held in June in Kananaskis, Alberta. I told John that all I was looking for at this meeting was a vote of confidence and some feedback on my quest for the commissioner's position. I wasn't asking to become commissioner right away, but I did want to know how I was doing and if I was on the right track. I also wanted to know how the board would react to John's decision and what actions they might take as a result.

Prior to the meeting, I thought it might be a good idea to meet with one of the governors who had been on the original search committee. I believed that this governor had been instrumental in the decision to reject me, and I wanted to know if our achievements over the past year had caused him to reconsider. Upon meeting with him, it was very clear that he had not changed his mind at all. As well, he made a few comments that I found quite disturbing. He asked me, "Why would you want to stay with the CFL? You'll never make any real money working for the league." He also felt it was necessary to tell me, "You realize, of course, that if you are to ever have a real shot at the job, you'll have to get rid of Geoff Fardy." This remark didn't make sense — unless he was trying to undermine my relationship with Geoff. I knew then and there that this man would never support me in anything. I also decided that I would never lower myself to ask for his support again.

As usual, the board discussed the issue behind closed doors in Kananaskis, and I found myself out in the hallway again, waiting like a child to find out my fate. Immediately afterward, John took me aside and explained that the board had decided that they needed more information and agreed to discuss the matter again at the next meeting, in August. In fact, they decided to dedicate one full day to the discussion. The most disappointing part was that the person charged with pulling the information together was none other than the governor who wanted me to fire Geoff Fardy.

Also upsetting was John's demeanour as he explained the results of the meeting. He was obviously agitated and upset.

I deduced from his behavior that the meeting had gone worse than he was letting on. I trusted John and knew that he was working to help me. I told him that, based on past behaviour, I no longer trusted the governors as a group. He looked at me and said, "Don't worry, I won't let them screw you."

The next few months were very difficult. There was a cold war of sorts going on behind my back. Perhaps I should rephrase that. In a war, there are two parties fighting; this felt more like a siege. The governor in charge of reviewing the governance issue was the main participant. To achieve his vision for the league, he felt as though he needed to change the leadership, which at that point meant me. In the months leading up to the August meeting, he gathered the information on leadership alternatives, as requested by the board, but, in my opinion, he set out to undermine and discredit me as well. At one point, he even called the league's auditor to ask some questions. The auditor called me afterward and described the conversation as "unusual."

Just prior to the August meeting, this governor called me to complain about what a poor job the league office was doing in the sponsorship sales area, saying that he was going to recommend a change. Naturally, I got upset and argued against his position with cold, hard facts that indicated otherwise. This governor then had a representative from his club call Geoff Fardy and suggest the same thing. The representative went one step further and told Geoff

that at the upcoming board meeting he was going to recommend that his own team take over all league sponsorship
sales. To illustrate just how twisted this idea was, this particular team had one of the lowest sponsorship sales of any
team in the league for the last two years running, which I
guess in his mind qualified them for the job. Upon hearing
about this second conversation, I immediately called the club
representative and told him to keep his ideas to himself.

The August meeting, held in Vancouver, was a two-day
affair. The first day was a full board meeting, while the
second day was set aside for governance discussions. The
lobbying in and around the board meeting was intense.
Contrary to my wishes, the governor and his representative
brought up their proposal to take over sponsorship sales.
Their original plan had been slightly altered: they didn't
want to take over all sales just yet, only Grey Cup sales.
Although they may have thought that this was in the best
interest of the league at the time, it seemed to me that the
main objective was to cast a shadow over my leadership and
to discredit my staff and me. In the end, they didn't get the
support of the board and the idea died.

I flew home right after the first day's board meeting, as
no staff members were to be present for the governance
session held on Sunday. On Monday night, I met with John
Tory at his home to discuss the results of the session and find
out my fate. John told me that the governors had decided to
initiate a search for a new commissioner, which he would

conduct in a very quiet and discreet manner. The board's objective was to have someone in place by the time of the Grey Cup in Winnipeg. John added that the board was happy with the job I was doing and that they wanted me to stay, but that I would not be considered for the position of commissioner.

I was expecting this result, so I wasn't all that upset. When I asked why I wouldn't be considered, he said that the board was looking for a "corporate blueblood" type: a person who could walk into any boardroom in this country and garner respect based solely on who they were. They also wanted someone who could handle the media. John told me that the board's decision was unanimous. He went on to say that in the opinion of the board, I didn't have what it took to lead the league to the next level. I reminded John that just two years earlier I was told that if the league could generate enough profit to distribute $1 million per club, we would be successful. I had achieved that goal in less than two years.

Now the governors had set a new definition for success: $2 million per club. I believed that I could achieve that as well. When I asked John why they wouldn't give me a shot at the commissioner's position, his response told me everything that I needed to know. Obviously John had anticipated this question, because he said, "When I asked the governors if they would consider making you commissioner if you could guarantee $40 million per club, the answer from

one team was 'No.'" John never told me which team governor it was, but I know in my heart who it had to have been.

It's important to know that I wasn't upset with John Tory
at all. He was simply the messenger, and I had a lot of experience delivering bad news, so I knew better than to blame
the messenger in a situation like this. I also knew that if it
were up to John, I would have been commissioner already.
Despite what John had told me about how happy the board
was with my accomplishments, the actions of that one
governor weighed heavily on my mind. His lobbying had
obviously been successful. The fact that the decision had
apparently been unanimous was very upsetting. Even if I
stayed on as president, how long would I last? I told John
that night that I would leave as soon as the new commissioner was appointed. My first inclination had been to pick
up and leave right then and there, but I didn't want to leave
the league in the lurch.

Over the next few days, calls from various governors
started to stream in. Two of them, in particular, told me
that the meeting in Vancouver was heated and divisive. I
was told in no uncertain terms that the vote had been far
from unanimous. I shared with them my decision to leave
as a result of the feedback I had been given. In response,
one governor told me, "Don't bother packing your bags, as
no candidate for commissioner will ever be able to get the
six out of eight votes required." One of the governors took
it upon himself to call many of the other governors and tell

them of my decision. Together, they demanded a meeting to discuss the situation further.

On August 25, 1998, the board held a private conference call to discuss the situation again. Afterward, one governor was asked by the board to call and speak to me. He reiterated John's comments about how happy they were with my performance and said that the board definitely wanted me to stay on. He confirmed much of what John had said about the kind of commissioner they were looking for — but he went a little further. He had the nerve to say, "We are looking for someone with the right family name."

John and I met during the first week of September to discuss my situation. John had just attended the sold-out Labour Day game in Hamilton the weekend before and came back with the realization that things were going very well throughout the league. He questioned why the league would want to make leadership changes at this point and asked if I would reconsider my decision. He proposed that everything would be left the same. The search for a commissioner would be called off, he would stay on as acting commissioner, and I would maintain my current role. After some thought, I said I was prepared to accept this proposal for one primary reason: I'm not a quitter. The league's turnaround wasn't complete, and I wanted to finish what I had started.

The majority of the governors agreed with John's proposal. We proceeded to complete the year as though nothing had happened. For the city of Winnipeg, the 1998 Grey Cup was only a moderate success, but overall the CFL enjoyed one of its best years in decades. The new television contract, combined with many new sponsors, meant that we distributed more money to the clubs than expected. The television ratings soared on both TSN and the CBC, and attendance across the league increased as well. There were lots of reasons to celebrate, and I was trying hard to focus on the positive.

17

The 1999 Season: Wrestling with Opportunities

During the winter and spring of 1999, while planning for
the upcoming season, there was a real sense of anticipation
and excitement in the league. The financial pressure was
less than in previous years, but a different type of pressure
settled in: the kind of pressure that comes from knowing
that despite all your achievements, you still have to do a lot
better. For anyone to do a job well, he or she must dare to be
different — raise the stakes a little and stand out from the
crowd. We had to have the confidence to set goals that others
would never dream of and to tackle new challenges. For the
CFL, it was time to become a little more revolutionary, in
the hope that others would follow.

We had doubled our sponsorship revenue in 1998, but that
was yesterday's news. Because of our financial difficulties,
there was an expectation that we had to double it again —
and we knew this would be twice as difficult. Our television

ratings had soared, which would be a useful selling tool, but we still had a couple of problem franchises. I was also starting to sense that we were about to hit the threshold with our corporate partners in terms of financial patience. To get to the next level, we needed to develop a long-term plan that we could all focus on. To my mind, this was a legitimate next step. The league had achieved its short-term goal of stabilization, but now it was time to forge a new vision. A vision that would take us from the survival phase into the growth phase. I was convinced that if the vision was powerful enough, our corporate partners would support us like never before and our success would be guaranteed.

In the first half of 1999, we also focused on sales and strengthening the weaker franchises. In particular, the Toronto franchise became a high priority, due to the owners' desire to sell the team. The team had unofficially been for sale for months, but very little progress was being made. The situation was creating a great deal of uncertainty in the league, so we decided to assist the owners in finding a buyer.

Sometime in early February 1999, through one of our mutual broadcast partners, I first became aware of the World Wrestling Federation's interest in the CFL. I called their Canadian president, Carl Demarco, and we met in Toronto for an open discussion of the opportunity in Toronto, among other topics. He had some interest in Toronto's club, but he was more interested in talking about the CFL in general. At the end of that first meeting, Carl said that the chairman of the WWF, Vince McMahon, probably wasn't interested in owning just the Toronto club, but he might be interested in the entire league. This didn't take me totally by surprise, but it certainly took our discussions to a whole new level.

The CFL had toyed with the idea of selling off a percentage of the league for years. The most common concept involved selling a percentage of CFL Properties — the entity that controls the television, sponsorship, and licensing revenue — through a legal arrangement with the CFL. In this model, the ownership of the clubs would not change, but the new partner would own a part of the cash streams generated by CFL Properties and, in turn, be represented on the board of the CFL. This idea was something that we revisited on a regular basis. It was time to dust it off again in light of the WWF's interest.

I decided not to share my discussion with Carl with anyone. As Carl requested, I put together a confidentiality agreement and an information package, in anticipation of meeting with Vince and Carl to further explore the opportunity.

Over the next few months, Carl and I continued to talk, and in April Carl invited me down to the WWF's head office in Stamford, Connecticut, to meet with Vince. I was told that they would send a car for me when I arrived at the New York airport to take me to their Connecticut office. Sure enough, a driver was waiting for me in New York, but he escorted me not just to a car but to the biggest limousine that I had ever seen. On the hour-long drive up to Stamford,

I had to yell at the driver if I wanted to ask him anything, since he was so far away. Eventually we arrived at the WWF office, which they affectionately refer to as Titan Towers. The four- or five-storey building resembled the kind of structure that a large bank might use as its head office.

My first impressions were very different from what I had expected. Except for some large, tasteful wrestling posters that stretched almost three storeys in height and the gorgeous WWF motorcycle that sparkled under the lights next to the elevators, the lobby could have easily belonged to any business. There were no scantily clad women or long-haired, muscle-bound wrestlers.

Before my meeting with Vince, Carl took me on a tour of the offices. What struck me was how integrated the business was. Within one building, they had a legal department, event planners, marketing, a travel department, finance, licensing, and Internet people. Everyone Carl introduced me to on the tour was very friendly — and very busy.

At one point, Carl introduced me to Shane McMahon, Vince's son, who occupied a tiny office in the midst of a group of offices. The night before, I had told my son, a huge WWF fan, where I was going. He said that if I saw Shane, I should ask him if there were any after-effects from getting hit with a shovel in last week's show. I did ask Shane, and of course he was fine. When I got home and told my son, he looked relieved.

The tour moved on to the production facility, a huge

building with heavy security, which was just a couple of blocks away. The first thing I saw was a training ring. I was introduced to one of the men who train the wrestlers to perform. He was reviewing a videotape from a previous training session and was critiquing the performance of the wrestler on the tape. As he answered my questions, I realized how much hard work and practice goes into what looks like a chaotic free-for-all. I also came to appreciate the amount of athletic skill required to make it look so easy.

Our next stop was the music studio. In keeping with their strategy of controlling everything, the WWF records all their own music on site with musicians they hire. This way, they don't owe anyone royalties, and they can control when and where the music is played.

Our last stop was their television studio. Every night, somewhere in the world, the WWF stages a live event. In some cases the event is broadcast live and in some cases it's taped, sent back to this studio, and made into a packaged show. The whole set-up was truly first-class and very high-tech. The facility included satellite hook-ups, studios, editing machines, and special effects technology that would rival even the most advanced television network. By the time I left the building, I had a whole new respect for the business acumen of Vince McMahon. I could hardly wait to meet him.

About an hour later, Carl and I met with Vince in his office, along with his wife Linda, the company's CEO. Vince struck me as a very quiet, thoughtful, and gracious man, one who was sincerely interested in football, Canada, and the CFL. Of course, this was completely the opposite of what I had expected, but I was getting used to the unexpected by now.

Because I still wanted the WWF to purchase the Toronto club – even though they had said that they wanted the whole thing – I had prepared a report outlining the history of the CFL. I also included some pertinent information about ratings, attendance, league and club revenue, and my views on why the WWF should get involved with the Toronto club. I didn't think that our owners would ever consider selling any part of the league to the WWF, but I was pretty sure they would accept them as owners in Toronto.

Despite my efforts to get him focused on the Toronto team, Vince continued to insist that he wanted to control the entire league. By the end of the 90-minute meeting, I had the sense that Vince understood more about our league and had a better grasp of the challenges involved than most people who had been involved with the CFL for years. His vision was clear and simple: he wanted to launch a new North American outdoor football league that would play in the fall, and he wanted the CFL to form the foundation for this new league. He envisioned eight teams in Canada and eight teams in the United States during the very first season. He had thought through the strategies and tactics, he had a marketing plan all laid out in his mind, and he was ready to go. The major issue for him was getting control of the television production. In his opinion, the game currently wasn't being presented the way it deserved to be. I left the meeting with the understanding that we would continue to talk and that Vince would probably come to Toronto in the near future to discuss the opportunity further and to meet with our major broadcaster, TSN.

On my trip back to the airport, I was overcome by a number of emotions. I was excited by the fact that someone other than me could see the potential in the CFL. After all those years of being the only voice preaching the virtues of a bold and aggressive vision for the league, it was nice to have someone else see the same thing. Perhaps his vision wasn't the right one for us, but the fact that he recognized the potentail in our league was a victory in itself. I wondered how the media might react if they knew what I was up to. It was important that I keep this initiative as quiet as possible, for a couple of reasons. First, I needed more time to flesh out details of the opportunity before presenting it to the governors. Secondly, if the discussions became public before I had a chance to tell the governors, I would be roasted.

Upon my return, I started to lay out the blueprint for structuring a deal that would satisfy both the WWF and the CFL's governors. The challenge was to come up with an agreement that would allow the WWF to feel that they had the control they were looking for, without really giving anything up. I was very conscious of the fact that the CFL is, after all, a Canadian institution that belongs to the fans, and I didn't want to betray that responsibility. On the other hand, if there was an opportunity to strengthen and build that institution with the assistance of the WWF, then it was worth considering.

In early May, I found out that Vince and his wife Linda would be coming to Toronto shortly, primarily to meet with TSN. Vince wanted to explore the idea of the WWF either taking over the television production of CFL games or, at least, working with TSN to improve the production. It was Vince's position that the CFL's image had to be significantly enhanced, and in his opinion the only way to do that was to invest heavily in the production of our games. Based on his experience, television positions the product and drives the business. Everything else is secondary. With the CFL, it was gate revenue rather than television that was the driving factor behind most decisions. Unfortunately, the need to maximize gate revenue had created an environment in which our teams viewed television as a necessary evil rather than an essential marketing tool.

Carl indicated that Vince and Linda wanted to meet with me again while they were in Toronto. I figured that this would be a good time to bring John Tory into the loop and add a fresh perspective to the proceedings. I met with John and filled him in on the developments of the past few months. Much to my surprise, he was fascinated by the whole idea. Naturally, he had a number of concerns, many of which were similar to mine, but I was encouraged by his open-mindedness. He had the same instinct about keeping the whole thing as secret as possible and not letting our governors in on it until the time was right — if there ever was such a time.

We met in the private dining room of a large restaurant. We all tried to keep a very low profile, but it was obvious that with someone like Vince McMahon that just wasn't going to be possible. The waiter who served us was beside himself with excitement, and as the lunch proceeded I noticed more and more staff peeking into the room. The meeting went very well. John and I both tried to convince Vince and Linda that they should start with owning the Toronto club and, if things went well, look at expanding their involvement later. Vince stuck to the position that he wanted to invest in the entire league. John was very direct and outlined the sensitive issues involved in such a relationship, but this didn't seem to deter Vince. We parted with the understanding that Vince wanted to proceed despite the challenges, and we all agreed to work together in good faith to see if there was a deal to be made.

We left the meeting separately so that no one would see the two top officials in the CFL leaving with Vince and Linda McMahon. I'm sure that if we had been spotted it would have been all over the papers the next day. From the restaurant, John returned to the office while I headed to a scheduled meeting with TSN. Vince, Linda, and Carl would be attending as well, but I was travelling separately from them.

I arrived at TSN first. As I waited in the lobby, I suddenly realized that there was no way that we could be seen together in this building, since the place was swarming with sports reporters who would have loved to break the story. As I sat there waiting to be taken upstairs, I heard Vince and the others coming down the hall toward the lobby. I quickly ducked out through a separate exit and waited in a washroom until I was sure they had left the lobby and were up in the private meeting room. I then returned to the lobby, where the receptionist looked at me as if I were an idiot. She didn't understand why I'd run out, but she didn't really care. She was still flushed with excitement from meeting Vince.

When we all met upstairs, we went over the broadcasting issues related to the WWF's potential involvement in the CFL. It became obvious that this was more than an exchange between an event producer and a broadcaster; this was an exchange between two broadcasters. As a result, there was a certain amount of professional competitiveness between the two parties. After a while, the conversation turned to how much money TSN could afford to invest in the production of the CFL compared to how much the WWF felt needed to be spent to meet the standards to which they were accustomed. By the time I left nothing was resolved, other than an agreement to continue discussions.

In just three weeks the CFL was due to hold a board meeting. John and I agreed that we would tell the governors about the developments with the WWF, but that we wouldn't identify the actual organization itself — not just yet.

18

Eventco?

At the board meeting of June 3, 1999, the governors were told that a worldwide entertainment company with extensive television and marketing capabilities was interested in making an investment in the CFL and expanding the league into the United States. I even came up with a code name for the company: Eventco. You could almost see the eyes of the private owners light up with dollar signs. The community-owned teams, however, were less than enthralled. After an extensive discussion that, disappointingly, focused more on the problems of such an investment than on the benefits, the board allowed the league office to continue with the negotiations. Despite repeated requests to identify Eventco, neither John nor I gave in. There were times in the exchange when we looked at each other and smiled as governors tried in vain to guess. They never even came close.

After the board meeting, I went back to Carl and indicated in writing that I had a mandate to continue the talks, provided Vince would agree to a few conditions. The board, not knowing with whom it was dealing, wanted Eventco to know that there were four non-negotiable issues. Eventco had to agree to maintain the salary cap, maintain the Canadian player quota, guarantee that the existing Canadian cities would always have a team, and make a commitment to revenue equalization so that all teams would be on the same competitive level. Vince and Carl verbally agreed to these basic conditions and confirmed that they would continue working toward an expression of interest letter. Once we had this letter, we would reveal the interested party to the board.

Things moved slowly over the summer of 1999. The WWF was in the middle of restructuring and was working toward filing their prospectus to go public. This took up a lot of their attention and focus during the next few months. The organization's attention was also diverted by the unfortunate death of wrestler Owen Hart, who died from a devastating accident during one of the WWF's events that summer. Despite all these diversions, both Carl and Vince kept in touch and we continued working together.

During this time, I continued to stress how important it was for the CFL to develop its own strategic plan. For the past few years, our plan had been simply to survive, but it was now time to look beyond survival and plan for growth and stability. In this new phase, we would probably have to make some tough, risky choices. These decisions would be much easier to make if we were all working toward the same goal. To achieve this, I arranged a strategic planning session for the board in early August. I was convinced that the league could have an exciting future, if we could take advantage of the opportunities being presented to us. I was hoping that the governors would find the courage to take a few risks and move forward boldly.

It was my hope that we would come out of the strategic planning session with a clear-cut vision for the new, reborn CFL. If our vision was in sync with what Eventco wanted to do, then great; if not, then we would put Eventco behind us and move on. I didn't want to tell the governors who Eventco was until we had forged this vision, for fear that it might sway their thinking one way or the other. Much to my dismay, and despite a great deal of effort by both John and me, this session concluded with nothing more, in my eyes, than a commitment to the status quo. It was the most disappointing day of my entire career with the CFL.

After it became obvious that we were going to leave the session without a new vision, John and I we decided to spill the beans and tell the governors the identity of Eventco. They were told that Vince wanted to invest in the CFL and use it as a base to launch a new North American football league, which would play its games in the fall. In my overview, I made it clear to everyone that Vince had decided to start a new football league one way or the other. If he couldn't reach an agreement with us, then he would start one on his own. I also told them that Vince was confident that he could negotiate significant contracts with U.S. broadcasters over the next few months.

Many governors were disappointed when they found out that Eventco was actually the WWF. They had convinced themselves that it was someone like NBC or IMG (International Management Group). Those who had no interest in the whole concept felt a sense of relief. If the potential partner had been NBC or IMG, the deal would have been much more difficult to ignore. Despite their disappointment, the board agreed to allow me to continue the discussions. Upon reflection, I think they allowed me to continue the talks purely out of curiosity. Even though publicly they expressed doubt about Vince's ability to get a new league off the ground, privately they were concerned and wanted to stay on top of him. Most of them had no intention of ever considering a deal with the WWF, no matter what was offered.

I was convinced at this point that the WWF opportunity was going nowhere, but I trudged on anyway. I was getting very frustrated – not because we were about to turn our backs on the WWF, but because I couldn't get the board to focus on the future. It's one thing to turn down someone with a vision that's not in sync with yours; it's quite another thing to turn someone down without having an alternative. The board seemed too divided along philosophical and egotistical lines to ever agree on anything, let alone a common vision. This situation was causing tremendous operational challenges for me. Perhaps more out of frustration than anything else, I decided to do an interview with Scott Taylor of the *Winnipeg Free Press*, intending to float a number of controversial ideas and generate some public discussion. The interview certainly did that, and more, as it was picked up by the media all across Canada.

The most controversial idea I suggested in the interview was re-examining U.S. expansion. I told Taylor that I had asked the governors what we, as a league, wanted to be when we grew up. I was then quoted as saying, "We've spent three years circling the wagons. We've made a lot of progress, but it's time to start planning for the future." The essence of the article was that we were at a crossroads and the decisions we made from this point on would determine whether we were successful. The article achieved exactly what I wanted it to do. It shook people up and generated a great deal of debate. The Internet chat rooms were humming with debate, as was my voice mail at work, which recorded the thoughts of many irate and upset people. I got the sense that some people would prefer to see the CFL die rather than ever see it expand to the United States again. I wasn't saying that U.S. expansion was the only possible strategy, but it was one strategy more than we currently had. Some people understood my point, while others saw it as a black-and-white issue.

I had hit a nerve, but it was a nerve that needed to be hit.

In this day and age, change is so prevalent and rapid that if you're not constantly changing, you're essentially going backward. It's possible to fall permanently behind in a very short period of time, and not even realize it until it's too late. This can happen to both individuals and organizations. When organizations reach this point, the result is, at best, major restructuring, or, at worst, insolvency and bankruptcy. The CFL found itself in this position at the end if the 1996 season because it got caught standing still for well over a decade. The complacency that began in the 1980s seemed to have intensified. For example, we continued to sit idly by as the broadcast world expanded and allowed the Canadian public greater access to a vast array of North American sports. I felt it was time to do something more.

On August 27, I again visited with Carl, Vince, and Linda at the WWF's head office in Connecticut. I shared with them the results of our strategic planning meeting and the challenges that we would face in structuring a deal that would be acceptable to the board. Recognizing that the league deal was all but dead, I tried to get them to focus on the Toronto opportunity. Again, this went nowhere. During the conversation, I asked Vince how he might promote a team from Winnipeg that was coming to New York to play. My concern was that the people of New York wouldn't care about a team from the north. Vince looked at me and said, "By the time I'm finished, the people of New York will hate everything about Winnipeg, and they will hate the team. That's how I will get the people out." I never doubted him and I never questioned the concept again. At the end of the meeting, despite my warnings, Vince insisted on putting together a letter that would outline his interest in the CFL and provide a timeline to explore the opportunity. This letter whould bring the issue to a head and get it resolved once and for all.

On September 3, in the midst of the swirling controversy created by Scott Taylor's article, I received the letter from the WWF and prepared to send it out to the governors. In the letter, Vince asked for an exclusive negotiating period. I thought this was reasonable, but I also knew that the board would have a hard time agreeing to this demand. Before sending it out, I discussed Vince's request with a couple of the governors and asked for their input. Their consensus was that the WWF should have to pay something for this exclusivity. It was not a position that I shared, but neverthe-less I agreed to pursue it. I spoke with Carl and Vince about the issue, and they said that they would give it some thought and get back to me.

I was in my car the next day when my cell phone rang. It was Carl, saying that Vince wanted to talk right away but he didn't like talking to people on cell phones. Would I consider finding a pay phone and calling them back? I called and we discussed various ways that the WWF could avoid paying for exclusivity. Vince was reluctant to pay any money, since no one else seemed to be interested in making an offer to the CFL. Vince came up with another way that he could help us financially, though indirectly, and at the same time demonstrate what a partnership with the WWF could do for the CFL in the future. He offered to stage, at his expense, a wrestling event during halftime at the 1999 Vancouver Grey Cup. Based on the cost and the quality of the entertainers, I was confident that this would be a great addition to the game. Not only would it likely sell thousands of additional tickets, but it would probably boost television ratings as well. It was certainly a creative response to the league's unwarranted request, but I didn't think for one minute that the governors would agree to this suggestion. I looked forward to telling the governors about it, as I was sure that their reaction would be interesting.

After settling the issue of compensation, I finally sent Vince's letter out to the governors and arranged a conference call later that week to determine if we wanted to continue the negotiations. The majority of the teams didn't want anything to do with a deal that involved the entire CFL. The next day, I informed Vince of the governors' decision. Needless to say, he was upset. In our final discussion, he said to me, "If they don't want anything to do with me, then I don't want anything to do with them. Just tell them that I will start my own league and I will bury the CFL."

I was happy that the WWF saga was behind us as it had taken up a lot of my time. It was obvious very early in our discussions that there was no deal to be made, but I did have a responsibility to run it to ground and provide the board with all the options. What this process did for me personally was reinforce and clarify just how much potential this league has. To achieve this potential, we must believe in the game and design a plan that will allow it to thrive, rather than simply trying to protect it. Without this plan or vision, the CFL will never achieve its full potential.

19

Behind the Scenes: The Politics Get Dirtier

Following our decision to pass on the WWF, and with other league developments in the ensuing months, I sensed that the split on the board concerning leadership was growing wider. By the end of the 1999 season, it was so severe that I doubted that we could agree on anything. On September 22, I wrote an open letter to the governors, pleading for co-operation and unification. The purpose of this frank letter was to urge everyone to get together, put personal differences aside, and step up to the challenge to remold and reshape the CFL. For a short period of time, it generated some discussion, but it was soon forgotten and we slipped back into our malaise.

This was frustrating. I believe that it is the job of every Canadian to take more responsibility for the future — the future of their business, the future of their country — but the CFL was not doing this. I wanted someone in the CFL to stand up and demonstrate that they gave a damn about

those things that are uniquely Canadian. The real challenge
for us was to reinvent ourselves and our business, so that we
could be better positioned to compete in the global market.
Although we couldn't control what would happen in the
future, we did have the power to control the kind of people
we wanted to be when we got there – the kind of people we
wanted to be when we grew up.

Now that the WWF was out of the picture, I had to get on
with finding a new owner for the Toronto team. Labatt, the
present owners of the Toronto Argonauts, had been trying
to sell the team for some time, without success. It was in the
best interest of the league to settle this issue quickly, so I
took it upon myself to help find a new owner. This began
with an extensive search for interested parties throughout
North America. There was a great deal of interest, but very
few people within Canada took a serious look at the opportunity. There were only two individuals who were prepared
to move forward and purchase the team.

Both of these potential buyers were American. That, in
itself, is a statement about the conservatism of Canadians
and our willingness to let other people take the responsibility for conserving something that is uniquely ours. In
the end, Sherwood Schwarz, a businessman from New York
City, bought the team and thereby ensured that the team
and the league survived to fight another day. Few people
realize the debt we owe to this man for stepping up when
very few others would – and no Canadians dared.

The 1999 season turned out to be one of the most memorable and successful in the CFL's long history. Attendance had increased again by over 5 percent, and our television ratings were up by almost 20 percent on TSN. Over two years, the TSN ratings had gone up almost 50 percent, with a large part of this increase in the under-18 age group. This boded well for our future. Again, sponsorships almost doubled. The league was able to replace the huge signing bonus obtained in 1998 from TSN with profit from operations, and again we distributed about $1 million to each team. The Grey Cup game was a huge success for everyone involved, and now a new owner had been found for Toronto. We were definitely on a roll, but new challenges on the horizon were about to burst our bubble. I used the media conference in Vancouver prior to the Grey Cup to once again warn that although the league was doing better, we needed to make some bold moves, or risk losing everything that we had accomplished. Again, this plea fell on the deaf ears of the governors.

It was clear to me that the league wasn't going to achieve its goal of financial independence without some major changes. We were close, but to continue narrowing the gap, we had to change our approach and make the CFL more relevant for today. I challenged everyone to concentrate on capturing the imagination of our fans as we entered the new millennium. I wanted us to set some *un*reasonable expectations, just as we had done when we doubled our sponsorship profit.

In setting unreasonable expectations – whether for an individual or for a business – an important question to ask is, What is the difference between what I am currently doing and what I know how to do? This answer to this question will determine both the scope of your aspirations and the likelihood of your success. As unpopular as the WWF was with our governors, the organization is a good example of this spirit of aspiration. Originally, the business consisted of a few staged wrestling matches in small-to mid-sized arenas across the United States and Canada. At some point, however, they realized that they were not just a wrestling business, but an entertainment business, and started to expand their business based on this definition.

The WWF then took the idea one step further. They integrated everything. Many people don't realize that the WWF has hundreds of people on the road at any one point in time, all around the world. To book all their travel arrangements, the WWF initially used their own in-house travel agency. Then they thought, why not create a separate travel company? The result is an outside travel agency through which WWF fans can book their holidays. Then, how about a football league? After all, it's consistent with being in the entertainment business and exploring new opportunities based on what they know. The WWF knows event marketing and broadcasting, and when you have a powerful brand and an area of expertise, why limit yourself?

In contrast, it is my opinion that the CFL is a great example of a Canadian business that has been limited by linear thinking. As it stands today, the CFL is viewed strictly as a football league, much like the WWF was originally just a wrestling company. The CFL's definition is further limited by the idea that it's a *Canadian* football league. Although the mid-1990s initiative to expand the league beyond its borders was far from successful, we could have used it as a learning experience. Many people, however, continue to point to this failed attempt as proof positive that it should never be tried again. In my opinion, it's this narrow, linear thinking and fear of failure that have to be changed.

At first I blamed myself for the do-nothing atmosphere that had taken over our league, but I eventually concluded that the philosophical split between the privately owned and the community-owned teams, combined with the various personality clashes among the governors, was the real root of the problem. The result was the worst possible result: the status quo. We didn't choose this result because it was the best option; we ended up with it because we couldn't agree on anything new or on ways to expand what we already had.

To further discourage any progress, the issue of league leadership had been completely ignored. To discuss strategic planning and not deal with leadership makes absolutely no sense. Again, we didn't deal with the matter of leadership because no one could agree on what to do – so we did nothing. The source of this paralysis was, in my opinion, the recent recommendation by John Tory that I become commissioner at the end of the year. The issue was so contentious that the board decided not to deal with it. Perhaps they thought that if they ignored the issue, it would go away. I knew, as most people did, that when you avoid dealing with a problem, the problem usually gets worse. Something had to be done.

I was pretty busy in the fall of 1999, as was my staff, organizing the playoffs and the Grey Cup in Vancouver. Finding Sherwood Schwartz had also been time-consuming, but to me it felt like proof that things could change. However, that season I received a call from one of the governors, who was known to be a fence-sitter on many issues, including league leadership. He called to "clear the air," as he put it, and started by saying that he thought I was doing a great job. He went on to say that it was a mistake for the board to have led me on all these years. In his words, "Some people are meant to be quarterbacks, and others equipment managers." He said that he would never try to convert an equipment manager into a quarterback or vice versa. After hanging up, all I could do was laugh. I was past the point of getting angry. I felt sorry for him; it was this type of outdated, egotistical thinking that contributed to the CFL's problems in the first place. Nothing worthwhile would ever be achieved until this kind of thinking was eradicated.

On November 2, 1999, I presented a detailed strategic plan to the board, outlining challenges and their solutions.

In this plan, I proposed a three-pronged approach. The plan focused on expansion within Canada as the top priority. Second, I asked for a substantial amount of money to invest in marketing and other activities. Finally, I proposed searching for a strategic partner who could provide money and open up new opportunities The plan passed. I'm certain that if I hadn't written my open letter to the governors in September challenging them to think boldly, this plan would never have passed so easily. Sometimes it takes time to see the fruits of your work.

20

The 2000 Season: In Other Arenas

With a new strategic plan in place — one generally accepted
by the board — things felt a little more stable. Still, I had
fears of new obstacles appearing on the horizon, and very
early in 2000 my fears were realized. First, the WWF
announced that they were going to make true on their earlier threat and launch a new league in 2001, the XFL. Within
the CFL, this news was greeted with a great deal of skepti-
cism. Most governors felt that it was just a public relations
move. It will never work without a television deal, was the
general sentiment. At about this time, news of our talks
with the WWF started to surface. The media wanted to
know what had happened and why. All that we said at first
was that the WWF and the CFL had indeed held talks, but
that they went nowhere. When it became obvious that the
story wouldn't go away, we admitted to more. We acknowledged that the talks had broken down because we couldn't

assure ourselves that the WWF would maintain the CFL as we knew it. We feared that our uniquely Canadian treasure might be lost forever under the WWF banner.

The threat of the XFL became even more serious when NBC became a partner with the WWF. Again, the reaction in the CFL was denial. It was my opinion that this development made the new league a legitimate contender and a force that we needed to be concerned with, whether the XFL was successful or not.

Feelings of uncertainty had become familiar by now, and we set out to launch the 2000 season as usual. A major advantage was that, for the first time, the league had a substantial marketing budget. Up until this point, any promotions or advertising was done on a shoestring, and it showed. I had convinced the governors to make the investment by persuading them that otherwise we wouldn't be able to increase our sponsorships or ratings much above the previous year's levels. The governors reluctantly agreed, but not before I personally promised to cover the additional investment with more revenue. In other words, the entire investment, with benefits that would accrue for years, had to be recouped within one year. I didn't think that this was reasonable, but I took a chance because it was the only way that I could get them to agree.

An integral part of our plan was the establishment of strategic alliances. One of these potential partners was the Arena Football League. I floated the idea of starting an arena league in Canada in conjunction with the AFL. Arena football is played indoors on artificial turf, and it tends to be a fast-moving, exciting game. Best of all, it takes place primarily in the CFL's off-season. The idea to work with the AFL was first hatched back in early 1999, when I met with the commissioner of the AFL and a number of their owners in Chicago. From there, we continued to talk and explore the idea further. We made arrangements for the AFL's commissioner, David Baker, to come to the Vancouver Grey Cup game and address our board. It was my hope that he would win over the governors and we could move forward to explore the concept more seriously.

I thought David's presentation was great. I was particularly impressed with his passion and energy, which flowed from a powerful vision for the league. He spoke about his product with an evangelical zeal that was dismissed by many of our governors as overly dramatic and too "Hollywood" in style. After he left, the general consensus – which I did not share – was that the AFL was an upstart league that wouldn't survive. The fact that the NFL had purchased an option in the AFL for millions of dollars was of no consequence to them. As far as I was concerned, however, the NFL's involvement gave the league a major credibility boost. The AFL was also assisted by the purchase of new franchises by some of the NFL's most powerful owners, including William Ford Clay, Jr., the owner of the Detroit Lions, and Jerry Jones, the owner of the Dallas Cowboys. The involvement

of the NFL and its owners paved the way for new sponsorship deals, extended television coverage, and more interest
in expansion franchises. The result has been a league on the
move. It has set its sights on expanding across North America, Europe, and beyond.

I continued to talk about the idea of a Canadian arena
league. To me, it seemed like a great way to expand the
sport, and I wanted to keep that possibility alive in Canada.
I hoped that talking about it as though it were a reality
might garner some new support. I was very impressed with
their vision, and so I kept in contact with David Baker and
the league representatives. The AFL representatives, however, were aware of the lukewarm response that their presentation had garnered in Vancouver and were concerned about
our ability to work together. I tried to assure them that there
was still an opportunity, though I wasn't all that convinced
myself. I didn't have a mandate from the board to initiate a
Canadian arena league, but nevertheless I continued to
believe in the idea – from both a defensive and an offensive
point of view.

On the defensive side, I was concerned that if we didn't
show real interest, the AFL would simply expand into
Canada without our involvement. This would be disastrous
for the CFL. If the AFL was hell-bent on being in Canada,
there wasn't much we could do to stop them, so we might as
well get involved and make the best of it.

On the offensive side, I believed that arena football was a

growing and viable business that was here to stay. If managed correctly, I felt that an arena league in Canada could help the CFL. In addition to promoting football year-round, it would allow us to promote our game in those parts of Canada where we had no presence, such as the Maritimes. If the playing season was January through June, rather than the normal AFL season, which is April through August, there wouldn't be any conflict with the CFL season. This would allow the CFL teams to reduce costs by allocating marketing and administrative staff to the arena league teams in the off-season. I hark back to the idea of growing your business based on what you know, not on what you do. The CFL knows football and it knows entertainment, so why not expand our business on this premise?

In the spring of 2000, the AFL launched their AFL2 league, which started with 15 teams. By early July, I had caught wind of an effort by a Toronto group to buy one of the existing AFL teams and move it to Toronto for the 2001 season. I called everyone I could think of – even the NFL – to see if we could stop this development, all to no avail. It seems that money speaks louder than words, and the Toronto group was paying a large amount for the franchise. Some of this money was going to the league but most of it was being paid to the powerful and influential Madison Square Garden group. The offer to purchase and transfer the franchise was to be discussed in August at the Arena Bowl in Orlando, Florida. I got myself invited to the meeting on the pretense

that I wanted to make a presentation about the CFL, but what
I really wanted to do was lobby against the proposed deal.

In advance of the meeting, I spoke with many of the
CFL governors about what position I should take. My initial
strategy was to be aggressive and outspoken about the negative effects of this development on CFL in general and the
Toronto Argonauts in particular. Naturally, Sherwood
Schwarz, the Argonauts owner, agreed with this approach,
but I was surprised at the reaction of a few other governors.
They believed that we didn't have anything to gain by
aggressively opposing the sale and we should take a neutral
position. How typically Canadian! I just couldn't understand
why anyone involved with this league would take such a
position, especially since it was contradictory to the interests
of their fellow governor in Toronto. It showed a total lack of
solidarity and specific disdain for the problems in Toronto.
Was there an underlying motive that I wasn't aware of?

I decided to stick with my original instinct and attended
the meeting with the goal of aggressively opposing the sale.
In my presentation to the AFL's board, I outlined the
progress we had made over the past three years and then
spoke about our desire to form a partnerhip with the AFL in
Canada. I said in no uncertain terms that if they agreed to
the purchase and transfer by the Toronto group, the chances
of such a partnership would be hurt.

Despite my pleas, the deal was approved. I didn't expect
anything else, since it wasn't really practical for the AFL to

turn down all that money and go against an organization as powerful as the Madison Square Garden group. Nevertheless, I was disappointed, as once again the CFL had missed an opportunity due to a lack of vision and foresight.

21

The Ottawa Initiative

Around April 2000, I also started the search for a new owner in Ottawa. Despite all the inherent benefits to expanding back to Ottawa, and the fact that it was included in the strategic plan they had approved earlier, the response I receicved from the governors on this initiative was lukewarm at best. The fear of past failures was still holding back many of them. I knew that without the board's full support, this endeavour was going to be much more difficult, but I was convinced that it was necessary. I acted as though I had their total support and launched the search, hoping that it would become a self-fulfilling prophecy. I wanted it to take on a life of its own. For that to happen, I was going to need the backing of the fans and the media in Ottawa and across the country. I would use this backing as leverage with the governors.

By June 2000, I had a letter of intent signed and approved by the CFL board of governors for the sale of a new Ottawa franchise to Grant White. Grant was a young entrepreneur, originally from Ottawa, who had started his career as an investment banker in New York and who, at the time of our negotiations, was the CEO of a publicly traded Internet company with its head office in London, England. Grant was an enthusiastic and motivated potential owner, backed by two wealthy American investors. The terms of the letter of intent were fairly detailed. All that we needed to do to complete the deal was arrange to lease Frank Clair Stadium from the region of Ottawa and agree on an expansion draft to stock the new team with players. All the other financial details had been settled. Over the next couple of months, Grant made himself available to the media and our governors whenever he was asked. He was often quoted in the media. His views on the future of the CFL were aggressive but sound. They were very much in line with my own views, actually. I know that this upset a few of the more conservative owners, who thought he was too brash.

Shortly after signing the letter of intent, both Grant and I attended the annual Rough Riders golf day in Ottawa. Many former players and media were in attendance. Grant was very accommodating and went out of his way to greet as many of the former players by name as he could. After the dinner, Grant was asked to say a few words. Before he did, he asked the media to leave the room so that he could speak with the players in private. The players loved him, and everyone left feeling great, full of confidence that CFL football would be back in Ottawa under Grant's ownership. The national media reported on the day and included various great interviews with Grant. Unfortunately, I sensed that a few within the league saw Grant as a threat, because if he did become an owner, the balance of power could shift and their influence might be diluted. As a result, I also sensed the wheels of influence begining to turn behind the scenes.

In early July, we held a board meeting in Toronto and invited Grant to meet the board and make a presentation. He was scheduled for 11:00 am, and had planned to fly in from New York the night before. When I arrived at the meeting that morning, I called his hotel to make sure everything had gone smoothly, but to my surprise he had not checked in and I couldn't reach him on his cell phone. I thought for a moment that perhaps he wasn't going to show, which would have been devastating. Not only was the media there, waiting to meet him, but a small clique of governors would have used this as an excuse to stop the entire process. At 10:30 am we took a break and, while I was standing outside the meeting room, Grant arrived. The New York airport had been shut down the previous evening due to lightning storms. When Grant couldn't confirm an early morning flight, he hired a limousine and a driver, driving all night, for a total of 10 hours, to make sure he arrived at the meeting. If that isn't commitment, then I don't know what is.

In the meeting the board asked Grant a few direct questions about his financing and future plans and he answered just as directly, which again riled a number of governors. Afterwards, I spoke with Grant, who felt that the board was trying to hold him to a higher level of scrutiny than they faced themselves. Grant could sense that something was wrong. He felt as though he was being attacked for being young and brash – the exact qualities that we needed. After the board meeting, Grant met with the media and spent almost an hour answering their questions. The response I got back from the media present was overwhelmingly positive. They loved the guy. This only served to anger the governors, who felt that they were losing control.

Over the next few months, there were various attempts to scuttle the deal by adjusting some of the terms of the agreed-upon letter of intent. To the surprise of many, Grant agreed to the revisions, some of which were quite substantial. By mid-August, Grant had a deal in principle for leasing the stadium and, by CFL standards, it was a deal to die for. All that we needed to agree on now was the expansion draft. A meeting with Grant and a select number of governors was scheduled in late July to finalize the details of the draft. During the process, a couple of governors attempted to again revise some of the financial terms of the original agreement, which made Grant very angry. But when he eventually calmed down, we agreed on the basic outline for an expansion draft and the new terms of the agreement.

I belive that Grant compromised more than he had wanted to in order to get the deal done, but he had already invested a fair amount of money in research and was anxious to get going. Assuming that the deal was all but complete, he continued to conduct research and interview potential candidates for the position of general manager of football operations.

The last step was to have the expansion draft approved by the players' association. Grant was aware of this requirement, but was led to believe that it would not be a problem. One governor made a vague comment to Grant that, as part of the draft proposal, the league would be asking the players' association to agree to a reduction in the number of Canadians on each team — but it was never suggested that this would be an obstacle. We left that meeting with the understanding that we had a deal, subject to the rubberstamp approval of the players' association.

As it turned out, the players' association didn't want any part of an expansion draft that would see the number of Canadians on each club's roster reduced, even by just one. As we discovered later, this had been a major point of disagreement between the league and the players' association during the last negotiation just two years earlier. The players had been so opposed to this development at the time that they had been prepared to strike over the issue. Knowing this, how could the key people responsible for player relations think that the association would give in this time? As I saw it, this was the tactic of last resort by the influential clique that didn't want the deal with Grant to go through. They knew that the players' association would never agree to the expansion draft if it included this clause. In other words, the rejection of the draft proposal was assured, and certain people in the league knew that in advance. I had no idea that this would happen, and I blame myself for not realizing it sooner.

After speaking with the president of the players' association, Grant decided just before Labour Day to withdraw his offer. The president had confirmed Grant's worst fears: the expansion draft would never be approved if it included a reduction in the number of Canadians on each team. Grant put two and two together and realized that he had no chance of ever being approved for a franchise. Of course, the league then tried to blame Grant for withdrawing and accused him of being impetuous. At one point, some people even suggested that he didn't really have the financing, and that that was why he pulled out. To my knowledge, this was never the situation, and the suggestion was very unfair to Grant.

Grant deserved to be treated better than he was. Some governors criticized him openly, while others treated him with complete disdain. In spite of having been dealt with in a rude and unprofessional manner, he had persisted because he believed in the product. At the risk of sounding cynical, I would contend that the average Canadian company — as represented here by the CFL — is typically unwilling to listen to new voices. Many of these companies are run by a stodgy

"old guard" who create new strategies in isolation and uni-
laterally reject revolutionary ideas that fall outside their
comfort zone. Sadly, some ideas are rejected for no other
reason than that they didn't originate in the corner office.
The CFL didn't just lose a great new owner and a potential
revolutionary – it created an enemy. We pushed out a man
who simply wanted to contribute to the future of the league.

Canadian companies that are on the leading edge, the
ones enjoying the financial benefits of the global revolution, have created an environment where new voices are
actively sought, fed, and nurtured, unlike the environment
that exists in the CFL. These companies know that all successful reinventions are led by revolutionaries. If the voices
of these revolutionaries are stifled or muted, then the reinvention will not occur. Providing revolutionaries with a
forum for their ideas is one secret to successfully preparing
for the future. Those organizations that are totally committed to this process end up creating the equivalent of an idea
marketplace, where ideas are treated like commodities and
entrepreneurs thrive.

Organizations and the people who run them should be on
the lookout for potential revolutionaries – who can come
from anywhere within the organization, at any level – and
be sensitive to their needs. Why? Simply put, revolutionaries
see things that others can't. They can see these things primarily because they are coming from a completely different
direction than most, with few or no prejudices about what

works and what doesn't. For this reason, young people tend to be a major source of revolutionary ideas. They are more in tune with what's going on in the world and where things are going. They live with new technological developments and work with them to a far greater degree than do the older generation, yet many refuse to listen to their insights. It's almost as if the so-called mature adults are overwhelmed with the progress of the last 10 years and are screaming for a time out so that they can catch their breath, while the young people are pleading for even more change.

Fresh blood is also vital to the development of new ideas. One current trend sees people skipping from one career to another. Many successful people are taking the knowledge and experience they have developed in one industry and transferring it to a totally new industry. These people come into the new industry with a clean slate, with no preconceived notions about how things should be done — only how they can be done better. Again, this only works when the people at the top have the courage to take a risk and reach outside their industry, looking for fresh ideas. They also have to be secure enough to defend their past practices and be willing to be questioned and challenged about their plans for the future.

Finally, we must not lose sight of the people who live on the edges of an organization. In a company with a lot of branches, it's the outposts that make great breeding grounds for revolutionaries. In companies with assembly lines, the

individuals to look out for are the workers who make the
products day in and day out. They are often much closer to
the customers or the products than anyone else, and therefore they know first-hand what customers really want or
what problems the product has. They know about red tape
and they know all the shortcuts as well. There is a lot to
be learned from these people, and they have a lot to say if
given the opportunity.

Sadly, the CFL doesn't work that way, and it did not listen
to a young newcomer when maybe it should have. This was
not an isolated case, unfortunately. In my time with the CFL,
I noticed a real reluctance to accept new ideas from people
who hadn't paid their dues, so to speak. In my opinion, the
"jock mentality" in the CFL prevents those who haven't
played the game from making any serious contributions. On
many occasions, I was reminded that I didn't play the game
and therefore didn't really understand what was involved
in making changes. There were times when I tried to push
the envelope and inevitably someone would push back with
sarcastic or disparaging comments. Others have suffered the
same treatment, I believe. This management style is not
productive; it has to change.

One thing that I've come to realize about the world of
professional sport is that common sense doesn't always pre-
vail. In fact, it seldom does. The world of professional sport
is all about ego and influence. I've spoken to enough people
in other leagues to know that this is not unique to the CFL.

Yet I would like to believe that the CFL should be above this. After all, it isn't just any professional league: it's a Canadian tradition that belongs to the people of this country. The team owners simply hold it in trust.

22

The Search for a Strategic Partner... Again

Having come up short with the WWF and the AFL, not to
mention the foundering attempt to secure a new owner in
Ottawa, I was starting to wonder if I could ever find a partner that would be acceptable to the governors. Nevertheless,
consistent with the plan that the governors had approved, I
put together a package and set out to find a strategic partner
who was prepared not only to invest in the league but also
to contribute non-financial, synergistic benefits that would
help us grow. It had always been my position that the
league was severely undercapitalized and that we needed an
investor who would provide much-needed capital to be used
in expansion and marketing initiatives. The most obvious
potential partners were the broadcasters in Canada, so that's
where I started.

By mid-2000, the convergence trend was well underway.
Media companies were either buying or merging with other

media companies to broaden their reach and complement their existing services. For example, BCE, which already controlled both conventional and cellular phone services in Canada through Bell, not to mention Internet services through Sympatico, decided to expand into the broadcasting business and purchased CTV, which by this time also owned TSN. BCE then arranged to purchase the *Globe and Mail* and a number of other communications products as well.

The objective was to control all the possible ways of communicating with consumers, which are often referred to as the communication channels. This was also the strategy followed by Rogers Communications, which owned a cellular phone business in Cantel, a form of broadcasting in Rogers Cable, many radio stations, magazines, and an Internet provider in Rogers@Home. CanWest Global, which was primarily a broadcaster, got into the act as well when it bought the *National Post*, among other newspapers, and launched its own Internet service.

The next development in this trend was that these corporate giants attempted to gain control over products – such as sports teams – that would provide content for their communication channels. Rogers decided to buy the Toronto Blue Jays, and rumour had it that BCE was looking to buy the Toronto Maple Leafs and the Toronto Raptors; an obvious opportunity was developing for the CFL.

I approached BCE, Rogers, and CanWest Global about investing in and owning a piece of the CFL, and I got some real interest. One party, in particular, was very interested and we proceeded to sign a letter of intent, which gave an exclusive period of negotiation. Once again, I had a difficult time getting the necessary approval from the governors, although negotiations were going very well with our prospective partner. I finally received the board's approval in late August 2000, right after the Ottawa deal fell apart and I announced that I was stepping down at the end of the season.

I should have realized that my mandate to move forward on this project was weak at best, but I thought that I could make it work. In hindsight, I believe I was given the go-ahead because no one thought that the talks would ever come to anything. This theory was confirmed when I informed the governors that we were about to enter the due diligence phase. Within a day, I was instructed to discontinue the discussions and tell the potential partner that everything was on hold until our leadership issues had been resolved. I was stunned. We were on the verge of a major business arrangement that had the potential to take the CFL to a whole new level, and I was told to stop – only weeks after I had been given the approval to proceed.

23

Behind the Scenes: The Final Straw

The unfortunate treatment of Grant White and the demise of the Ottawa initiative was the last straw. Despite the progress that I was making with our prospective strategic partner, I decided to resign right after Labour Day, effective December 1, 2000. The behind-the-scenes politics of that year best explain why I chose to move on.

It was no secret that governance had been an issue for many years, but the situation hit new lows in the first six months of 2000. The story begins when our first board meeting of the year was cancelled for lack of interest. I say that tongue-in-cheek — the truth is that the only thing that people were interested in was leadership. The problem was that everyone was too apprehensive to bring it out in the open; hence, no meeting.

Complicating the situation was the fact that one of the governors had taken it upon himself to conduct a private search for a new commissioner. Some of his activities made it into the press, which angered many of the other governors. I constantly got calls from the other governors, wondering what he was doing and questioning his mandate. To my knowledge, no one challenged him directly.

The next scheduled meeting, in February, was also difficult to bring together. At the last minute, everyone reluctantly decided to attend. As was our custom, John Tory and I met before the meeting to discuss the issues. We both knew that the topic of leadership would have to be addressed, but we certainly didn't expect what was about to unfold.

The meeting started at around 6:00 pm and was scheduled to go until 11:00 pm and then continue the next morning. Around 11:30 pm, John suggested that I and the other CFL staff leave the room, so that the board members could discuss governance. Out in the hallway, we sat and paced until the meeting broke up at 1:00 am. All the governors headed to their rooms without saying much. John, to his credit, sat with me for about 15 minutes, explaining the events of the past hour and a half. He was visibly upset.

The governors had decided to conduct a search for a new chairman and CEO and eventually a new commissioner. Supposedly, once the new chairman was in place, he would determine the appropriate structure and the best role for me. I was quite honestly surprised and upset — not for myself, but for John. After all those years of being a volunteer chairman, seeing the league through some difficult times, this was a real slap in the face. Was this the price for having supported me for years against great opposition?

The meeting reconvened the next morning. About half an hour into it, I asked John if I could address the board. My message was simple but emotional. After my speech, a few questions were voiced. Then, total confusion reigned as everyone started talking at once; there were obviously two distinct camps in the room. Once again, I was asked to leave while they fought this out in private. After an hour, I was invited back in and told that they would have a conference call the next week to discuss the topic further.

The conference call was held about a week later. Afterward, I got a call from one of the newer governors, who had been asked by John and the board to relay the results to me. As I understood it, someone had nominated me for commissioner, with five governors voting in favour and three against. The CFL's constitution requires at least 75 percent of the votes for the motion to pass, which means I needed six out of eight votes. The governor expressed to me how disappointed he was. In his words, the rationale of the people who voted against me made no sense. He went on to say that he, along with the other four governors who had voted for me, wanted me to stay on. He explained that John would call with what he thought was an attractive proposal. He concluded by saying that the search process was on hold indefinitely.

John called the next night to express his frustration with the entire situation and propose an arrangement that would have me stay until the end of the year. He confirmed that the search was on hold. The irony of it all was that the board could vote to give me a pay raise with a simple majority (five out of eight votes) and it could vote to prevent a search to replace me with a simple majority, but it couldn't make me commissioner with only five votes. I decided to stay for the balance of the year, but I promised myself then and there that this would definitely be my last year and that I was going to go out with a bang.

Everything was relatively quiet for the next few months, which for the CFL didn't mean that all the internal fighting had stopped — just that the media wasn't picking it up. I initiated the search for a new owner in Ottawa and we all put our noses to the grindstone to successfully launch another season. There was a board meeting scheduled for early May, which would be only our second meeting of the year, as well as our annual general meeting. There were a lot of great things happening across the league that we needed to discuss.

About 10 days before the scheduled board meeting, I got a call at home from one of the governors, who proceeded to tell me that he had polled the governors and the consensus was that the May meeting wasn't needed. He had two reasons. The first was that he and a few others couldn't make it. The second was that he wanted to avoid a problem. He said that, in his opinion, John Tory didn't have enough votes to get re-elected as chairman. He mentioned that he had spoken with some other governors who also shared this opinion. He asked me to poll the governors the next day and arrange to have the meeting cancelled. Before ending our conversation, he asked me how many votes John would need and I said six. He responded, "Then I don't think he has the votes," implying that he, along with at least two others, would vote against John.

The understanding at this point was that John had agreed to stand for re-election as chairman at the upcoming meeting for the balance of the 2000 season only. After that, he would step down after eight great years and dedicate his time to some other worthy endeavour. It was obvious that this governor was not satisfied with that arrangement. The next day I called a number of governors and shared the gist of the conversation with them. All of the governors I spoke with knew about this governor's position, but no one knew where the other two votes would come from. Most of us concluded that he was bluffing.

The May meeting was cancelled because no one wanted to deal with the controversy at that point. Over the next few weeks, a few governors continued to beat the drums of discontent. The media picked up on the controversy and were playing it for all it was worth. Following a particularly negative article on May 23, I spoke with John. He sounded upset and he was taking all the back-stabbing very personally. He referred to it as a conspiracy.

At about this time, I was still hopeful about the prospects for a new Ottawa franchise, with Grant White as an owner. But turmoil had erupted when I had asked for permission to move forward with the letter of intent. In response to my outline of the proposed deal, which had been sent out to the board members on May 19, I had received letters from two governors, one suggesting that I didn't have a mandate to negotiate a deal and the other suggesting that there was an imbalance between the initiatives of the league office and the authority granted to it. Both of these positions were totally wrong: I had received the authority to proceed with the Ottawa deal at the February board meeting.

In response to this disturbing turn of events, John and I held a conference call the evening of May 23 to deal with the situation in Ottawa. There were some suggestions about how the deal might be improved, but there was no real opposition from anyone on the phone. Following the call, I went ahead and renegotiated some of the terms. In the meantime, one of the two discontented governors spoke to the media in Ottawa, saying that I wasn't the best spokesman for league expansion. After that comment, I decided that it was time to take the gloves off.

Over the next two days, I talked with most of the governors about the revised terms for Ottawa, asking them all to step up and defend both John and me publicly. My point was that private support was great but, in the wake of the public attack by certain governors, private support was no longer good enough. On Thursday, May 25, I sent out the revised terms for Ottawa and asked the governors for their consent to move forward. By Friday night, I had the backing of six governors, which was all I needed. On Monday, the CFL announced that it had an agreement in principle with Grant White to sell him a new franchise. The way in which that deal subsequently collapsed (The Ottawa Initiative), and the fact that the whole affair alienated Grant, simply added to my fears that the antagonism could not be resolved.

The next board meeting was held on June 16, and when it came time to discuss governance, I was asked to leave the room, along with the rest of the staff. This was the first meeting that John missed in over six years. Based on the feedback from various governors who came and went during the discussion, the main focus of the closed meeting was not me, but John Tory. I found out later that John had informed the board that he was prepared to stay on in his position for the rest of the year, but only if the board unanimously approved his reappointment. After six hours, the governors finally emerged with what they said was a unanimous vote. I was told that there had been no discussion of my situation, other than the fact that a search committee had been formed to look for a new chairman.

On July 6, I met with the head of the search committee, who told me that the committee was thinking of looking for a commissioner before finding a chairman. He added that it would be a public search, conducted by a headhunter, and that he and a few other governors wanted me to submit my name. I let him know that I would not apply. Because of that, he recommended that the search be delayed until sometime in the fall.

Around July 10, I started to get a little suspicious about why the search had been switched from one for a chairman to one for a commissioner. My suspicions were further aroused after a conversation with one governor who, when I asked for his support, responded, "There were some deals made at the June board meeting which may make that difficult." Later that day, another governor spoke to me privately and said, "You didn't hear this from me, but there was a deal made at the June meeting. In order to get the support of the full board, there were assurances that there would be a public search for chairman, and I think commissioner as well."

After this conversation, I called the head of the search committee and asked him if there had been a deal. He didn't acknowledge anything at first, but he called me back later, saying, "There was a deal made but it didn't involve you, and that's all I can say." He then tried to encourage me to apply for the commissioner's job, implying that if I did, I would have the support of five clubs.

Later in July, another governor informed me that he had taken over as head of the search committee and that he would then be in charge of hiring the search firm. In his words, "Whether you apply or not, you will be the leading candidate." I got the distinct impression that the search was about to begin. I told John Tory about these comments and asked him to ensure that if a search did start my contract would be honoured for the balance of the year. He assured me of this and added that the search committee was considering starting the search early — although they knew that, for business reasons, I was very much against this. My greatest concern was that a public search would create an air of uncertainty at a very critical stage in our selling season. That, in turn, could negatively affect our year-end results.

It was mid-August before I went on a holiday. During my time off, I decided that I would announce my resignation soon after returning. I could have stayed and fought through the threats of another search for a commissioner; I could have even thrown my hat into the ring. But the bottom line was that I was tired, and I had reached the point where I could no longer be effective. To cement my decision, John Tory was leaving at the end of the year. I just couldn't imagine continuing the fight on my own.

I announced my resignation right after Labour Day, and the search for a commissioner kicked into high gear.

24

24

A Radical Future

To the public and in terms of business, 2000 was a banner year for the CFL. Television ratings were way up again and net sponsorship revenue had increased by almost 20 percent. Attendance had increased across the league, and the 2000 Radically Canadian marketing campaign was turning into a huge success.

The league had maintained the Radically Canadian theme to some degree ever since 1996, but in recent years we had decided to refocus our efforts. For the 2000 season, we decided to relaunch it and redefine what being Radically Canadian was all about. We wanted to celebrate the uniqueness and unpredictability of our game, qualities that we firmly believe make it a better game than...that other one.

Molson's "I Am Canadian Rant" was at its peak, which we could use to our advantage. With our advertising agency, we came up with the idea of taking a roving camera onto the streets of America and asking average Americans what they thought about the CFL and our unique rules. The theme was "Radically Canadian: we play by our own rules."

The results were funny and informative. For example, we asked women in New Orleans if they knew that the CFL had an extra man on the field and unlimited motion in the back-field. The response was something like, "You can never have too many men and the more motion the better." We asked a man in New York for his reaction to the rule about no fair catches. His response was, "Wow, that must be dangerous. I hope you have a lot of aspirins on hand." We asked what people thought of the fact that there are only 20 seconds between plays, to which they responded, "Wow, that's a lot of action – your players must be a lot smarter than ours."

Soliciting the views of Americans was a risk in itself; people wanted to know why we would use Americans to promote a Canadian game. The answer was simple and speaks to the main insecurity we have in this country. First, Canadians never really believe that anything we have is any good until America tells us it is. Secondly, Canadians are far too close to the CFL to see it for what it really is. We needed to let Canadians see how others view our game, in the hope that those comments would force us to take a second look. I've said it many times before and I will say it again: in my experience, Americans look at the CFL and other Canadian businesses and see potential. It was time for us to see the same potential.

Reaction from both the media and the public was over-whelmingly positive. People were talking about the spots everywhere I went. The ads achieved the goals we had set and they helped us redefine what being Radically Canadian meant. I'm not suggesting that the Radically Canadian theme deserves to be voted into the advertising hall of fame, nor am I suggesting that the two Radically Canadian campaigns created the kind of real change that makes a lasting difference. But what these campaigns did was to effectively brand the CFL as a unique Canadian product and give the league a new, more aggressive attitude. We broke a few rules and took a great deal of risk to get the campaigns off the ground, but it was well worth it. The CFL has had to break rules in the past to get to where it is today, and I hope that it will break many more in the near future.

To do that, the CFL needs to be receptive to change. While it has the potential to become a revolutionary business, there are many obstacles to overcome. There is no doubt that the CFL has the most important element for a success-ful revolution: a worthwhile cause. For those who are close to the league, the cause is clear and compelling. The CFL has very deep roots – far deeper than any other professional sport in this country. That's because the CFL is more than a sport. The game of Canadian football has become an inte-gral part of Canadian culture.

The Grey Cup game continues to draw record numbers of Canadians to their television sets every November – not only to cheer for their favourite team, but also to celebrate a great Canadian custom. Similarly, the three major Labour Day games sell out on a regular basis, because they have become cultural markers for the end of summer and the start of a new school year.

As if preserving this history and tradition isn't cause enough, the CFL is also Canada's only indigenous professional sport played exclusively in this country. Add to this the fact that half the positions on every team are reserved for Canadians, which is also unique in the world of sports, and the result is an organization with a powerful cause that carries with it a sense of responsibility. The CFL is the quintessential example of Canadian tradition and pride.

And while I gladly acknowledge the CFL's bold breaking of a few rules, I also believe that, overall, the league has not implemented any real change for decades – primarily because it has become a victim of its past and of the expectations of its fans. The league is struggling with the challenge of remaining loyal to the traditions of the past and yet becoming relevant in the future. The same traditions that have made the CFL what it is today are getting in the way of its future. The closest that the league has come to real change – change that broke the rules – was its attempt at U.S. expansion. Unfortunately, many people refer to it as the biggest mistake that the league has ever made. Was U.S. expansion really a bad idea? It may have been a great idea poorly executed.

The CFL has failed to successfully reinvent itself, and it is suffering the consequences. The league desperately needs to break a few more rules in order to move forward and become a truly Radically Canadian company that we can all be proud of. Expansion into the United States was an effort to break the rules, but it was an isolated effort and it failed. Since then, the CFL has shied away from any bold new moves. In the future, the league needs to find the courage to go out and make these bold moves.

It is my opinion that the attempt at U.S. expansion created a fear of failure in the CFL. One of the key conditions for a successful revolutionary business is an environment where taking risks is encouraged. This can only happen in an organization that isn't afraid to fail. The U.S. expansion effort was a classic case of allowing the opinion of others to influence decisions about the future. The negative publicity surrounding this venture was immense. The media and others labelled the effort a failure, which it was, because it fit the classic definition: it was poorly executed and suffered the same mistakes over and over again. The public opinion was that the little CFL was way out of its league in trying such a bold move, and hopefully it had learned its lesson. I'd like to counter that by saying the plan failed not because it was a bad idea, but because it wasn't given a fair chance to succeed. The league should have learned from its mistakes, regrouped, and forged ahead. Instead, it retreated and hid. That's not the reaction of a revolutionary organization.

That's the reaction of a business afraid to fail again. The CFL desperately needs to find the courage it had back in early 1992, when it started this initiative, and take some bold new action. Its future depends on that.

I was speaking to a group about the future of the CFL just last summer when this point really hit home for me. After my presentation there were lots of people with all kinds of ideas, most of them very positive. During my speech, I had mentioned that over 50 percent of our viewers on TSN were over 50 years old. One man, who had been a big CFL fan all his life and who fell within that 50-plus demographic group, stood up and made a very interesting comment. He said that it was time to forget about the older group and start marketing the league to a new generation of fans. He added that the older generation would probably disagree with our approach but that we shouldn't really care, since most people of his age were diehard fans who would follow the game regardless of what we did.

His point was that we needed to take a few risks in order to move the CFL into the new millennium. These moves will inevitably meet with resistance from the older generation of fans, but if we truly believe in the cause, then that's a risk we need to take. The CFL definitely has the main ingredient for becoming a Radically Canadian company: the cause is clear and powerful. Everything else needs improvement. The league has to reinvent itself. It can be done. All it needs is the will — and the people — to make it happen.

For six long years, I tried my best to be a Radical Canadian in the true sense of the term. The personal benefits have been many. In addition to the sense of satisfaction that comes from making a difference, the skills and experience I've gained have been very valuable. What gives me the most satisfaction is that I remained focused on the cause despite the politics. Perhaps because of these efforts, I'm as committed today as I ever was. The personal benefits of a commitment to a worthwhile cause are not limited to the CFL. There are many other causes that need champions. I encourage you to find one and find out for yourself how rewarding it can be.

I took some risks and they were worth it – maybe I should have taken more. During my tenure with the league, ratings were up 80 percent on TSN, sponsorships increased by about 300 percent, distributions to the teams exceeded $20 million, and the league was once again relatively financially stable. Did I achieve my goal? No, I didn't – I didn't transform the CFL into the vibrant, viable business that it once was and still could be. But, as they say, the only mistake is a mistake made twice.

Over time, and despite strong effort, it had become obvious that I no longer had sufficient support to keep the league moving forward. It was time to step aside and allow someone else to lead the charge. When I decided to resign, I had no idea what I would do next. I planned to take some time off and then start looking, but I should have known better.

25

A Great Cause: The Source of Real Change

Like me, Sherwood Schwarz, the owner of the Toronto
Argonauts, had a tough year – but for different reasons.
His management team made many mistakes and, as a result,
they lost the support of both the media and the fans. Attendance dropped to unprecedented levels and the club lost a
great deal of money. As the season drew to a close, Schwarz
was beside himself with disappointment and was looking
for a way to turn things around. I was impressed by his
commitment. Most men would have turned and run after
such an experience, but not Sherwood. He wanted, more
than ever, to change things and start anew. This attitude
was inspiring.

As I neared the end of my time with the CFL, I started to
consider helping Sherwood with the Toronto challenge.
Most importantly, I felt a tremendous sense of responsibility
to him. I was the one who had sold him the team and I felt

as though I had an obligation to try to fix the problem.
As well, I had always thought that one of the keys to
permanently fixing the CFL was fixing its biggest and most-
watched franchise. The Argonauts, after all, play in Canada's
biggest city, the home to most of our country's major corporate head offices. This is where the decisions regarding
advertising and sponsorship investment are made. For this
reason, corporate Canada's perception of the CFL is greatly
influenced by how the Argos are doing. In my opinion, the
CFL will never reach its full potential until the Argos are
successful, and I wanted to help make that happen. My earlier idea of taking some time off went by the wayside.
When I resigned from my league position, I became president of the Toronto Argonauts.

As I see it, the fight is not over yet. All I've done is
change tactics. Writing this book is one of those tactics,
which I hope will make a contribution to the overall goal as
well. I've come to realize that, in the business of sports,
phrases such as "a good offence is the best defence" are no
longer empty clichés – they are fact. The truth is that for
anything – be it sports or business – to grow and prosper, it
must be able to change. The adoption of a cause is where it
all begins. Everything else flows from this step. It's the core
belief around which every action is focused and every decision is made.

Adopting a great external cause begins with determining
what's important to you. Over the past 10 years, I've spoken

to many organizations on various management topics, most of which have centred on change management. I've also spoken to many groups on the topic of personal career management. Whether my focus was the corporation or the individual, the theme was basically the same. It always dealt with change, particularly the need for individuals to become agents for change. In trying to help people understand this concept and then put it into action, I came up with the term "inside-out leadership."

Inside-out leadership is about learning to lead yourself before attempting to lead others. And it's about changing yourself before trying to change others. Lead by example – never expect anyone to do something that you're not prepared to do yourself. Therefore, you must set high standards for yourself and others. Carry yourself with confidence, always produce a first-class product, and demonstrate a flawless work ethic. This means working more hours than you have to, always being on time (early is better), and always looking professional.

The real leaders in our workplaces are those who believe in themselves and know what they want – they lead by example. When it comes right down to it, leadership is all about self-confidence, self-esteem, and a commitment to self-improvement. These are qualities that you can't force on people. You can't demand that they get passionate and you can't force them to be confident. These are 0qualities that people have to give themselves. In the work environment, it is these personal qualities that enable a person to attack change, to take risks, and to lead others. People who have tapped into these internal energy sources attract others like magnets. The key to tapping into these sources of energy and passion is the commitment to a personal cause.

Ask yourself, Am I a follower or a leader? And more importantly, Which one do I want to be? Since the key to becoming a leader in the traditional sense of the word is to learn how to lead yourself, you must be driven by a powerful personal cause or vision. Let me explain what I mean by a personal vision with a personal example.

Whenever I come upon a situation or opportunity that requires me to make a decision, I apply what I call my rocking chair test to it. I close my eyes and picture myself sitting in my rocking chair, long after I've retired. One of my many grandchildren is sitting on the floor beside me, asking questions. These questions are about my life, my experiences, my career, and the choices I've made. As only young kids can, my grandchild is asking blunt, straightforward questions, with none of the guarded politeness that adults tend to use. With every answer, there is the inevitable follow-up question, "Why?" In answering these questions, my goal is not to use the words "I should have" or "I could have." My personal cause is to be the best person I can be. To me, this means living up to my full potential and being a good father and husband. I determined years ago that to achieve these goals, it would be necessary to take more risks than normal, so that I can avoid having to use phrases such as "I could have" or "I should have." My personal cause is to be the best that I can be, and not leave anything on the table when my time is up. This cause drives me, and every decision I make is centred on it. To achieve this, I seek out synergistic and extraordinary opportunities that will contribute to this goal. In most cases, this requires setting unreasonable goals and following through to achieve them.

To a typically conservative, risk-averse Canadian, setting unreasonable expectations is the equivalent of jumping into the deep end of the pool without knowing how to swim. Few people are bold enough to dream of what might be. We've been programmed to set reasonable goals – goals that make sense – and to keep our feet firmly planted on the ground. But that's exactly the kind of thinking that got us into this problem in the first place. With feet firmly planted on the ground, how can we expect to get *off* the ground?

All around the world, there are companies and people setting unreasonable goals and achieving them at unreasonable rates. For these businesses and the people behind them, there are no borders, only customers. They don't care that Canada's a separate country with its own economy and a unique infrastructure designed to support our treasured social programs. All they see is a large, lucrative, receptive market waiting to be dominated. For these global companies, capturing the Canadian market is but one step in a global strategy and one small part of their overall strategy for achieving their unreasonable expectations. It's nothing personal; it's just business, and there are no rules. Canada cannot compete if we continue to set merely reasonable goals.

For businesses looking to capture the Canadian market, we've been a very easy target. The most common criticism levelled at the average Canadian company is that it isn't aggressive enough to compete effectively with the American invasion. Canadian companies have been accused of being far too risk-averse and far too conservative and complacent to put up a good fight. This has to change.

I see the CFL as one of those Canadian organizations with a huge inferiority complex. It continues to play Canadian-style football as if it were an island unto itself, completely ignoring the competition, the developments in the world of sports, and the changes in our own country. The CFL appears to be content with sitting back and waiting for the inevitable, which is the expansion of the NFL, the AFL, or another league into Canada. Even if these other leagues don't expand into Canada in the near future, their ever-growing presence in North America is putting real pressure on the CFL. The demand for our players and coaches is increasing. The growing broadcast penetration of our competitors in the Canadian marketplace serves only to dilute the CFL's fragile fan base.

The league's recent strategy, born out of the failed U.S. expansion effort, was to sit back and play it safe. This reaction isn't unique to the CFL — in fact it pervades our country, and I see such a reaction as very dangerous. It is a reaction that invites those terrible words, "I should have" or "I could have." But we can't live our lives in hindsight. Canadian companies have got to stop being so damn passive and start fighting back. The truth is that we have nothing to fear and nothing to feel inferior about. Whether we're talking about the CFL or any other Canadian business, it's time to get more aggressive and make it a fair fight.

The first step is to make setting unreasonable expectations a standard business practice in Canada. By their nature, unreasonable expectations force people to do things differently. Anyone can achieve a 5 to 10 percent growth in business with little or no change in their basic business strategies, but to achieve 50 percent growth requires reinvention and radical new strategies. Bold, unreasonable expectations create an expectation for innovation; and for such expectations to be effective, they have to be made public — that's one thing that the CFL has taught me. When we had to double our profit in 1999, we put the 100 percent increase in our 1999 budget, distributed it to the board, and agreed to have our bonuses totally dependent on attaining it. Geoff Fardy was certainly up to the challenge as he reinvented our sales and service policies and forced us to change the way we approached our business. All this provided crucial motivation and leverage.

Setting and ultimately achieving unreasonable expectations breeds pride and passion: two attitudes that can eradicate our current inferiority complex. Let's think big and dare to dream. Let's allow ourselves to be successful. One of the secrets to improving self-esteem and confidence is allowing oneself to feel successful. One of the best definitions of success that I've ever heard is this: "Success is the progressive realization of a worthy goal." This definition reinforces the importance of having a cause that drives you. It also emphasizes that success is not only the destination but also the journey. Setting and striving to achieve unreasonable goals is, in itself, a measure of success. Allow yourself to feel successful and you will be.

I believe that passion and enthusiasm are critical to your success on a personal level as well. If you're not enthusiastic about what you do, then you're not likely to be very effective. It is sad to see people struggle to cope in an organization — not because they can't do the job, but because they can't get excited about the business. This was not the case for me: the CFL was a perfect match. Its history and its role in Canadian culture were powerful motivators, and the Grey Cup game is a tradition that pulls this country together once a year. It reminds us what being Canadian is all about.

I put up with a lot during my six years at the CFL, but I never lost sight of the cause: to restore the league to a position of relative financial strength and prepare it for the future. I had a passion for the CFL. The one thing that drove me through all the personal attacks was that I truly believed that we were making things better for an institution that I really cared about. Going back to that definition of success, we were making progress toward a worthy goal. I urge you to find your own worthy goal and go for it.

26

Lessons Learned on the Journey

My time with the CFL was often intense and stressful. When you're in the middle of a situation like that, it can be difficult to focus on anything other than just surviving. The challenge is to step back and look at the big picture. It's a mistake to get so caught up in the day-to-day efforts to survive that you lose sight of your long-term objective. For the CFL, the long-term goal was restoring the league and making it a strong and vibrant business. When I was able to step back, I gained a number of significant insights from my experience, all based on common-sense business principles. The lessons I learned with the CFL changed my outlook. As a result, they have added some spark and some courage to my actions in the last few years. They will continue to influence me both personally and professionally for years to come.

While I won't suggest that we did everything right after the 1996 season, our accomplishments over the next four years were significant, and there is no doubt that we made major progress toward our long-term goal. I attribute a good part of that success to a commitment to change and a willingness to learn from past mistakes. As a result, the league is arguably much stronger than it has been in decades, but it is still far from being fixed. The league is still fragile and simply can't afford any major setbacks; I am convinced that it won't survive another look into the abyss like it had in 1996. It is my hope that the people now in charge of the league will continue to push for change and that they will develop new and extraordinary expectations for the league, all the while following solid, basic business principles. I believe that this strategy is worthwhile for all Canadians and Canadian businesses to keep in mind as they struggle to cope with the new economy.

All too often, businesses and the people who work in them change only when they are faced with no other option. On the business front, it often takes a calamity such as severe financial distress to force organizational change. On the personal side, it's events like a demotion or, worse, dismissal that force real change. Often, by the time we get to this point, it's almost too late. To be in control, to head off unexpected calamities like this, we must implement change strategies that will ensure that we're constantly growing and learning.

To evolve, we must ensure that we engage in lifelong learning. This may be as simple as reading books or taking courses. It also involves recognizing that one of the greatest sources of information is the experience of others. The XFL, for example, has folded. What lessons can the CFL learn from that league's experience? It is my sincere hope that the CFL doesn't point to the XFL's failure in order to justify maintaining the status quo. This would be a real mistake, for I continue to believe that there is room in North America for another outdoor professional football league. If the WWF doesn't run it, then someone else eventually will. My question is, Why shouldn't it be the CFL? I think that is an extraordinary expectation that's worth pursuing. Let me explain why I feel this way.

The NFL has recently expanded to 32 teams, and most people believe that it will stay at this number for many years. All the major U.S. television markets (except for Los Angeles) now have a franchise. Expansion beyond the current markets will add very little to the NFL's ratings, which means at the moment they have optimized their television revenue with the existing 32 teams. In addition, the number of teams divides nicely into four divisions of 8. Each team is guaranteed an opponent every week which means there are no "by" weeks. No more teams are needed. The NFL also has no burning desire to expand into Canada. Again, it comes down to economics, which for the NFL means television. Adding a team in Canada would do nothing for U.S. ratings, and what little money they could get from a Canadian broadcaster would be offset by the cost to the existing teams of splitting the current television revenue with another franchise. It just doesn't add up. As the NFL's commissioner said just a few years ago, expansion into Canada isn't even on the radar screen.

If you assume that NFL expansion will be very limited over the next decade or so, then many first-class U.S. cities will be without any professional football. The AFL is attempting to fill this void by bringing its style of indoor football to many of these locations, with the support of the NFL. The AFL, however, is unable to fill the need for outdoor professional football in the fall. In my opinion, this represents a real opportunity for someone. Could that someone be the CFL?

There are many U.S. locations near the Canadian border with sufficient knowledge of our country and our game, where CFL-style football might just have a chance: places like Portland, Oregon; Columbus, Ohio; and Syracuse, New York, just to name a few. Columbus and Syracuse, for example, both have large universities with great football traditions. They could build new, professional teams around their university programs – teams stocked with alumni players who would draw fans and attract local corporate support.

What's the major obstacle to making this unreasonable expectation a reality? The answer is our inferiority complex. We're afraid that Americans will not accept our game without major changes, and so we prefer to sit back and do nothing, even though our game is slowly dying right before our very eyes. It's as if we're ashamed or embarrassed.

People say to one other, "Look what happened the last time we tried that." Or, "We tried that once before, and boy did we learn our lesson." That kind of talk is short-sighted. All we learned last time was how and where not to do it. The truth is that CFL football is a better game. All we need to do is convince ourselves of that fact and get on with it.

If you believe that the CFL can continue to exist as a Canadian-only league, then any discussion of U.S. expansion is unnecessary at this point. If, on the other hand, you believe that it either won't survive or, at best, will continue to struggle if it continues as an exclusively Canadian league, then the risks of U.S. expansion don't seem all that great. What is important is that football continues to be played at a professional level all across Canada and that there is a professional league for Canadian kids to play in, if that's what they want.

Football isn't the only sport in Canada that is struggling. Professional sport in Canada is under attack from all sides. Canada has already lost two NHL teams in Quebec and Winnipeg, and in all likelihood will lose more shortly. Professional baseball will disappear from Montreal very soon, and the Vancouver Grizzlies of the NBA are as good as gone. Where does this leave the CFL? It leaves the CFL with a great opportunity to show the way.

In my opinion it's naive to expect the CFL to continue to exist under its current structure. It is my position that the CFL needs to take on a partner and aggressively expand its product, first in Canada and then in the United States, with that partner's financial and strategic assistance. The most likely partner is the NFL. The U.S. league could work with the CFL to facilitate both U.S. and Canadian expansion of outdoor football, similar to their arrangement with the AFL. Failing this, the next most likely partner is a major Canadian communications company or, perhaps, even a major U.S. communications company. The AFL, while maybe not an ideal partner, could help as well, I believe.

I would propose that the following should be an integral part of such a relationship. First, all eight existing franchises (and hopefully Ottawa) must receive assurances that they will have a place in the league for at least 25 years, with all league revenue split evenly with all clubs – regardless of market size. Second, Canadian teams in the league should receive special compensation for the development of Canadian players, and a mechanism must be developed that will ensure that each Canadian team carries at least 10 Canadian players, without being at a competitive or financial disadvantage. Although it's not critical that all the CFL rules are maintained, I see no reason for them to change. I do believe it is important that the spirit of the Canadian game is protected and that the Canadian teams continue to have leverage in the league. The spirit and values of the CFL and the essence of "wider, longer, faster football" are what's really important.

As we consider expansion, there are a number of lessons

to be learned from the XFL experience. The first is that you cannot arbitrarily change a sport's season. Football is played in the fall, and that's when the fans expect to watch it. The Super Bowl marks the official end to the football season. At that point, people appropriately turn their attention to other sports, such as basketball and hockey. The XFL was hell-bent on playing in the major television markets, the same ones in which the NFL plays, and the only way the XFL could do that was to play in late winter and early spring. What they failed to recognize was that the television viewers in these markets had no real reason to tune in to their games. There was no loyalty or recognition factor among the viewers, and they were tired of football by that point. The CFL has already acknowledged this fact: it plays in the fall.

Second, people expect their sports to have a high degree of integrity and professionalism. According to many knowledgeable people in the CFL, the level of play and the execution level of the XFL was pretty good. Unfortunately, the marketing of the game betrayed the game on the field. The people behind the XFL tried so hard to be innovative that they went too far, actually taking away from the game by focusing more on the gimmicks and the activities around the game. This made the game itself look very amateurish and turned people off. The CFL, however, has made great efforts to maintain its integrity and history.

Finally, the XFL abandoned one of the key marketing strategies that worked so well for the WWF. The WWF, the

NFL, and the NBA are successful because they market their stars well. There were no stars in the XFL and, in fact, the league went out of its way to suppress their potential star players by putting too much emphasis on the activities around the game. The CFL, or whoever takes another shot at a new league in the United States, should keep this in mind.

When it comes right down to it, the CFL isn't any different from any other Canadian business. It doesn't enjoy any special rights or protection. It must learn to survive and prosper on its own. It must earn its right to exist day in and day out. The decisions faced by the CFL, especially the ones involving expansion, are the same ones facing most Canadian companies. I encourage those who run Canadian businesses to bravely reach out and develop unique, unreasonable expectations that extend beyond our borders, so that we can ensure Canada's place in the new global economy.

For the CFL and for many other Canadian businesses, the key to success is strategic alliances with like-minded organizations. Let's not worry about what we might lose in the process; let's expand and grow aggressively – let's focus on creating something we can all be proud of. If we insist on maintaining the status quo for fear of what we might lose, we risk losing everything. This country and its businesses need people to stand up and help guide us into the future. I encourage you to be one of these people. To start, simply find yourself a cause that will drive you. A cause that will allow you to stand up with courage and passion for the things you care about. A cause that will turn you into an agent for positive change.

I've often been invited to speak to various groups on the topics of change and career management. After each session, I would hang around and talk with people one on one. This gave me an opportunity to find out why they attended the seminar, what other seminars they had been to, and what they hoped to get from these sessions. I was surprised to discover that most of them were active seminar attendees, frequenting, on average, up to three or four a year. In addition, they all read extensively about their area of interest. I came to realize that, despite the wide variety and number of seminars and courses available, only a small percentage of the population actually takes advantage of these opportunities. This means that with just a little extra effort you can stand out from the crowd and make a real difference.

On a number of occasions, people came up to me after a presentation and told me that my remarks had helped them put things in perspective. Comments of this nature meant a lot to me, as they confirmed the importance of sharing one's experiences with others. These comments also made me realize how necessary it is to reach out and help more people. The opportunity to expose more people to the benefits of lifelong learning and career development, by using my experiences in the world of sports as a framework and a drawing card, was an incentive for writing this book.

In this book I've focused on the need for a grassroots

revolution to deal with the challenges faced by our country. The magnitude of these challenges means that our governments, our teaching institutions, and our businesses must support the revolution as well. We need to create an environment that encourages Canadians to stop and ask, "What if?" One that helps people turn their "what if's" into solid, concrete businesses. To achieve this, we need risk-taking that overcomes fear of failure. Thinking outside the box and questioning the status quo should be expected. People must be creative and innovative, rather than simply processors of information.

Creating this environment is critical for Canada and its businesses. Both are in desperate need of reinvention and a new generation of leaders who can lead us through this difficult period and into the new economy. We need to take advantage of our major resource — our unique and vibrant Canadian spirit — and build that spirit into everything we do or make. We have to stop worrying about what we might lose in this new world we're facing and focus on what we want to be when it arrives.

In telling the recent story behind the CFL, I have tried to focus on our attempts to fight against the complacency and apathy surrounding the league and on our attempts to implement real change between the 1997 and 2000 seasons. I hope, in the end, that you will learn from my mistakes and from my successes. Most importantly, I hope that you will get a sense of how much work is required to implement change and how much personal risk is involved. As long as you play the game with honesty and integrity at all times, in the end you'll be a better person for having tried, regardless of the results.

This isn't the end. My hope is that this is just the beginning of an exciting new phase for our country, its businesses, the CFL, and all of us personally. Many more chapters remain for us to write. We're at a crucial stage, and each of us is integral to the cause.

A Personal Thank-You Note

Although many people contributed to the CFL's success over the years, one person deserves special mention. I was lucky enough to work with John Tory, the chairman of the CFL, throughout my 6 years with the league. Prior to my joining the league, John had served as chairman for about 4 years. In total, he served the CFL as a volunteer for over 10 years. Obviously, John believed in the cause.

I was fortunate to have John as my mentor, and I'm proud to say we became good friends. Through all the trials and tribulations detailed in this book, John was beside me. He supported me whenever I asked, he ran interference when required, and he pushed through things that might never have been achieved otherwise. Without John's even mix of diplomacy and assertiveness, our board meetings — and perhaps the league — would have completely fallen apart. John kept everything together by ensuring that we all stayed focused on the cause.

It is my opinion that John Tory is the quintessential Radical Canadian. Since his departure from the league, he runs one of Canada's largest communications companies; he also devotes himself tirelessly to helping others through various charities. He cares about his community and his country and is actively involved in politics. When you consider all of this, his devotion to the CFL is truly inspirational. Without John Tory, this book could well have been about the demise of the CFL, and not its future.

Index

Adidas, 114

Alabama, 48

Alberta Treasury Branch (ATB), 65

Anderson, Fred, 46, 47

d'Aquino, Thomas, 21–22

Arena Bowl, Orlando, 156

Arena Football League (AFL), 153–55, 157–58, 193, 200, 202

Arena Football League (AFL2), 156

Auburn, 48

Baker, David, 154–55

Baltimore franchise, 34, 42, 47, 75

Baltimore Stallions, 43–45

B.C. Lions, 6, 34, 45, 68–69, 71, 73, 75, 76, 78, 80, 86

BCE, 170

Bell Canada, 170

Birmingham club, 36–37, 39–40, 42, 45–46, 48

Bishop, Lynn, 109

Budweiser, 98

Buffalo Bills, 97

Business Council on National Issues, 21–22

Calgary franchise, 34, 43, 68

Calgary Grey Cup 2000, 1, 6, 31, 102

Calgary Stampeders, 44, 66–67

Calgary Stampeders Football Club, 65

Camp, Walter, 27

Canadian Football League (CFL), 149, 197

and alliance with NFL, 94–95

chief operating officer/chief financial officer, 2–5

Flag Football Canada program, 96

polls, 16–18

regulations, 12–13

rules of the game, 29–30

sponsorship, 92–102

strategic planning, 137–38, 150–51

Canadian Rugby Union, 26–27, 30

Cantel, 170

CanWest Global, 170

CBC television, 111–12, 115–16, 125

CFL Properties, 128

Chen, Horn, 40, 43, 72–73, 75, 79–81, 94

Cherry, Don, 51, 74

Clay, William Ford, Jr., 154

Clemons Michael "Pinball", 6

Cleveland Browns, 45

CTV Sportsnet, 111–12

CTV television, 111–13, 115, 170

Dallas Cowboys, 154

Davis, Bill, x

Demarco, Carl, 127–28, 134, 137

Detroit Lions, 154

Edmonton Eskimos, 93

Edmonton Grey Cup 1997, 93,
    101–2, 110, 114

Edmonton team, 33–34

Estefan, Gloria, 99

Eventco, 136–44

Exhibition Stadium, Toronto, x

Fardy, Geoff, 87, 98–99, 114,
    119–20, 194

Farson, Richard, 58

Federal Express, 37

FedEx, 58

Firestone, Bruce, 36

Flag Football Canada program, 96

Forté, Mario, 77–78, 80

Frank Clair Stadium, 160

Global television, 111, 113

Globe and Mail, 2, 105, 170

Goldfarb Consultants, 17–18

Gregg, Allan R., 21

Grey Cup, 31, 33, 111, 183–84
    cost to stage, 85

origin of, 30
    See also Calgary Grey Cup;
        Edmonton Grey Cup; Hamilton
        Grey Cup; Vancouver Grey Cup

Grey, Lord Earl, 30

Gutsche, Sig, 67–8

Hamilton Grey Cup 1996, 84–91

Hamilton Ticats, 34

Hamilton Tiger-Cats, 34, 96–97

Hart, Owen, 137

ICF Consulting, 22

Jones, Jerry, 154

Kananaskis, Alberta, 118–19

Kelly, Jim, 39–40

Labatt's, 98, 146

Lansdown Park, Ottawa, 4

Las Vegas franchise, 34, 36

Liberty Bowl Stadium, 38–39

Lyman, Ted, 22

McCarthy, Mike, 75–76, 78

McGill University, 25

Maclean's magazine, 16–18, 22

McMahon, Linda, 130, 133–34, 141

McMahon, Shane, 129

McMahon, Vince, 128–35, 137–38,
    141–43

McMurtry, Roy, x

McNall, Bruce, 116

Madison Square Garden group,
156, 158

Management of the Absurd
(Farson), 58

Memphis franchise, 37–38, 42–43,
45–46

Molson's, 98–99, 181

Montreal Alouettes, 19–20

Montreal franchise, 34, 47, 73,
75–76, 80, 86, 93

MuchMusic, 111

National Football League (NFL), 10,
12, 31-32, 90, 94–96, 154–55,
193, 199–202, 204

National Hockey League, 13–14,
201

National Post, 170

NBA, 201, 204

NBC television, 153

North American football league,
138–39

North American Free Trade
Agreement, 14

Old Dominion University, 46–47

Ottawa club, 36, 42–43, 64,
79–82, 86

Ottawa franchise, 40, 71–72, 73,
94, 159–68, 177

The Ottawa Initiative, 178

Ottawa Rough Riders, 4, 34, 75–76

"Our balls are bigger", 51, 54–55

Pan-American Games, 115

Parkdale Canoe Club, 30

Passaglia, Lui, 6

"Practice With The Pros", 96–97

Princeton University, 26

Radically Canadian
marketing campaign 2000,
181–88
slogan, 8, 23, 50–56, 57–62, 74,
76

Regina Grey Cup, 43–44

Revenue Canada, 80–81, 86

Rogers Cable, 170

Rogers Communications, 170

Rogers, Pepper, 38, 43

Rosedale Field, Toronto, 30

Rugby Football Union, 25

Rutgers University, 26

Ryckman Financial Corporation,
65, 66

Ryckman, Larry, 43, 65, 67

Sacramento franchise, 34, 36

Sacramento Gold Miners, 46

San Antonio club, 42, 46, 47

Saskatchewan team, 33–34

Schwarz, Sherwood, 146, 150, 157, 190

Shreveport franchise, 34, 40, 42, 46

Skalbania, Nelson, 68–70, 71, 73, 75, 76–77

Skydome, Toronto, 6

Smith, Fred, 37–38

Smith, Larry, 53, 66, 73, 83–84, 91, 104, 107

Smith, Ted, x

Stevenson, Al, x

The Strategic Counsel, 21

Super Bowl, 31, 203

Super Bowl, Miami 1999, 98, 100

Sympatico, 170

Tagliabue, Paul, 94

Tampa Bay Buccaneers, 36

Taylor, Scott, 140, 142

Tim Hortons coffee chain, 87

Toronto Argonauts, 6, 34, 116, 146–47, 157, 190–91

Toronto Blue Jays, 170

Toronto club, 127–28, 131

Toronto Maple Leafs, 170

Toronto Raptors, 170

Tory, John, 6, 94, 104–9, 118–24, 133–35, 136, 150, 173–78, 180

TSN cable, 111, 113, 116, 125, 132–35, 147, 170, 186

UCLA, 38

United States Football League, 38

University of Memphis, 38

University of Toronto, 25, 30

U.S. expansion, 42–49, 140, 184, 193, 201

regrouping from, 63–70

Vancouver Grey Cup 1994, 34

Vancouver Grey Cup 1999, 143, 147, 150, 154

Vancouver Grizzlies, 201

Virginia, 46

White, Grant, 160–64, 172, 177–78

Williams, Arthur, 36–38, 39

Winnipeg franchise, 34, 43

Winnipeg Free Press, 140

Winnipeg Grey Cup 1998, 114–15, 116, 118, 122, 124–25

World Wrestling Federation (WWF), 127–35, 139–43, 146, 148, 152–53, 199, 203–4

XFL, 152–53, 199, 203

Yule, Dave, 6